Justified?

Justified?

◆

Questioning Military Indoctrination

Nadine Forbes

Writer's Showcase

New York Lincoln Shanghai

Justified?
Questioning Military Indoctrination

Writer's Showcase
an imprint of iUniverse, Inc.

For information address:
iUniverse, Inc.
2021 Pine Lake Road, Suite 100
Lincoln, NE 68512
www.iuniverse.com

First published 1999 by Pastime Press, a division of CICA Industries, Inc.

ISBN: 0-595-26234-1

Printed in the United States of America

I dedicate this book to my best friend, Nicole.
Thanks, big Sis, for your support, confidence, and unconditional love.

Contents

A special thanks to my editor and friend Sherry Noel Johnson for being so generous with her time. Her skill and gentle persuasion are all that any writer could ever want in an editor. Sherry, you are a true professional.

Abbreviations

ACT:	American College Testing
APFT:	Army Physical Fitness Test
ASVAB	Armed Forces Vocational Aptitude Battery
AWOL:	Absent Without Leave
BDU:	Battle Dress Uniform
BRM:	Basic Rifle Marksmanship
CIA:	Central Intelligence Agency
CPHQ:	Command Post Headquarters
G-10:	Group of 10-Belgium, Canada, France, Germany, Italy, Japan, Netherlands, Sweden, United Kingdom, and United States (original members.)
GNP:	Gross National Product
IMF:	International Monetary Fund
IMS:	International Monetary System
JCF:	Jamaica Constabulary Force
JDF:	Jamaica Defense Force
JLP:	Jamaica Labor Party
LZ:	Landing Zone
MASH:	Mobile Army Surgical Hospital
MEPS:	Military Entrance Processing Station
MOS:	Military Occupational Specialty
MP:	Military Police
NATO:	North Atlantic Treaty Organization
NCO:	Noncommissioned Officer

PNP: People's National Party

PT: Physical Training

PX: Post Exchange

R&R: Rest and Recreation

Foreword

As a soldier I encountered countless cases of blatant gender discrimination, abuse of power and sexual violence, and at a tender age began questioning the overall civility and justification of such institutionalized behavior. I have since dedicated my life to the fight for equality and due justice, not just for women but people of color, gays, and lesbians. Through my literary work, I hope to bring awareness to prejudicial thinking and behavior, and stimulate discussion on volatile issues of idealistic philosophies. I challenge conventional thinking and thoughtless rhetoric, and wish to present to you the raw reality of our present society from the vantagepoint of a military insider.

I have recognized a complex, societal, governmental, and political problem, and feel compelled to hold up a mirror for the world to take a good hard look. Ask yourself, "Are my actions, political voice and social posture pure and unbiased, or are they smothered in hidden agendas, crippled by fear, masked by ignorance and fueled by rage?" For God sakes, THINK!

1

Justified?

I started writing this book several years ago. My initial motivation was personal closure, however noting the ever-present media influx of sexual harassment charges and court martial cases, I have renewed impetus for completing this book. While writing, many questions arose relating not only to the military, but also to government and international policies. I will address specific situations and allow you, the reader, to answer for yourself where you stand. Are these policies justified?

Recently, I heard of a case where a drill sergeant inappropriately touched, and consistently harassed a recruit. The government was "investigating" these allegations. Those around me were shocked and appalled. My reaction on the other hand was indifference. "Is that it?" "Why all the fuss?" It was then that I realized that those who have not served truly don't know the real story of life in the military. People around me really don't know what the female soldier faces every day of her enlistment. People don't know the residual effects that manifest through those of us who are now out of the military and trying to cope with "normality," with family, with trust issues, with relationships, and with acceptance.

Although very young and zealous at the time, if I had known the real story, I am sure I would have reconsidered my decision to enlist. If my parents knew the real story, I am certain they would not have signed my life into hell.

I am thirty-five years old. It has been eighteen years since I took the oath to defend my country against all enemies foreign and domestic;

yet the experience in uniform still haunts me. I use the word *haunt* because it is like a dark, ever-lingering cloud that hovers over almost everything I do and see. It smells foul and the memories it harbors are choking. Seemingly innocuous every day things, like certain facial expressions, aerial sounds, '80s music, alarms, bugles, newspapers, trucks, hair styles, children's toys and games, the colors of green and brown, the occasional movie, and even the sun, sweat, rain, and specific cigarette brands all make me extremely tense and anxious. I guess some might say that I need to seek professional help, and indeed I have done so. Still, I feel in writing about my experience, I may enlighten you, the reader thus giving you an insight into the modern army you might never experience otherwise. You can, then, make informed voting decisions. You can make informed and appropriate decisions when thinking of enlistment. You can inform your daughters of what to expect before they take the oath, and better be able to communicate and empathize with friends who may be carrying an invisible, yet quite painful load.

The Army is a part of me now. It has permeated my being. The career choices I made, my temperament, my hobbies, my posture, my taste in clothes, the condition of my flat, my tolerance and expectations of friends, colleagues, subordinates and clients all stem from my brief exposure. I have asked myself on several occasions, who would I have become without 'time in.' Certainly, I would be quite different, but how? Hmm.

Let's begin with a simplistic breakdown of the organization of the United States military. Militaries as a whole were formed to frighten others into submission, to acquire land and resources, to spread ideology, to protect the weak, and yes, to ultimately defend against attack. The U.S. military has seven major branches: the Army, the Navy, the Air Force, the Marine Corp, the Coast Guard, the Air National Guard and the Army National Guard. In today's military, there is so much overlap of mission and purpose (i.e. Navy aviators). Nevertheless, the Army customarily deals with on-land assaults, the Navy with assaults by sea, the Air Force contributes by way of the sky, the Marine Corp. deals with amphibious attacks, and the Coast Guard protects the seas off our coastal borders. The Army National and Air National Guard are state militia and are controlled by governors; however both are subordinate to the U.S. Army when federally activated.

In all service branches there is very strict protocol regarding who's giving and who's following orders. Generals take orders from the highest uniformed commander, the Chairman of the Joint Chiefs of Staff, who answers only to the President. Colonels carry out orders from Generals but they give commands to Majors and Captains. Lieutenants, the lowest of the commissioned (or commanding) officers, take orders from the whole lot of them. Commissioned, or commanding officers, wear their rank and insignia on their shoulders to signify the "shouldering" of responsibility. Noncommissioned officers like Sergeant Majors all the way down to buck Privates wear their rank and insignia on the arm signifying the muscle or strength required to get the job done. So, it follows, noncommissioned officers carry out orders from the commanding officers mentioned above. Noncommissioned officers are Sergeant Majors, First Sergeants, and Master Sergeants. They give orders to the lower enlistees like Staff Sergeants, Corporals and Privates. Even a lowly Private (if a platoon leader,) can give orders to the squad leaders and squad leaders to the troops, but these kinds of orders must have definitely come from the higher-ups. This protocol for giving and receiving orders is called "the chain of command." Common phrases you hear often in the military are "…just following orders," or "Soldier, I gave you a direct order."

Intentions and purposes move through the House and Senate, where they are molded into missions. Missions metamorphose into orders to those in uniform. At that point, these orders are no longer up for debate.

This is where I shall introduce the terms; *obedience*—carrying out a command; *discipline*—control exercised over people; *and consequence*—result of what has gone before. These three terms are inextricably interrelated. Follow me on this one please. For a mission to be a predicable operation, thus giving the highest probability of success, the individuals directly carrying out the mission must unfailingly follow the plan crafted by the strategists. These strategists are trusted to be experts in intelligence work (knowledge of enemy resources, enemy strategies, weather, terrain, elements of surprise, allied support, etc.) The most expendable or the most easily replaceable people, usually the individuals with lower level skills and with less specialty training, are the ones put first in harm's way. Therefore, the "expendables" are most likely to impulsively abort the plan or alter it to serve their own best interest. These are the soldiers that must, above all, demonstrate *obedience*.

It is here where the term "discipline" comes into play. Discipline goes far beyond the parade field or palace guard gate. Discipline gives the assurance that the least expendables (strategists/officers, those more highly skilled and trained) need in order to guarantee obedience. Have I lost you yet?

Ultimately, officers need a unit of conformists. They need to have control. They need those under them to be absolutely submissive to commands. To help insure conformity, strict penalties for defiance are harshly enforced. Defiance may result in shame, imprisonment, humiliation, injury, or even death. The consequences must be harsh enough to be an undesirable option. For shame to be effective, one must first believe in the cause. Hence, failure to uphold the cause renders loss of one's unit and self-respect. It is right about here that the thinking person begins to question, does discipline really come from fear of consequence, or does it come with training? If so, how much training? Does it come with "sense of duty?" Where the Hell does sense of duty suddenly come from? How far can you push someone before they defy an order and resort back to self-preservation? What does it take for someone to completely surrender self? We'll get to that.

In addition to the mindless following of orders, another extremely important aspect of military objective success is public opinion. Consider our history as a nation. The only conflict in which we were unsuccessful, (Vietnam) was partly a failure due to revelation of the truth and methods of achieving the mission to an undoctrinated and naive civilian population that were highly emotional. Nor were they educated in the tactics and realities of war. Granted, there were other reasons for military failure in Southeast Asia; reasons like terrain, tenacity of the North Vietnamese forces, and the pre-adult age of our foot soldiers. But I am concentrating, for now, on the effects of public opinion. Hear me out, please.

North Vietnam aided by Communist China, invaded South Vietnam, a democratic nation with geographic and trade interests with the United States. Many of our Asian-based businesses made Vietnam their home and although there were workforce exploitations, goods were made available here in the USA for reasonable prices. Let us also not forget that many Vietnamese people were, at least then, employed, and therefore, could feed their families. In the process of invading South Vietnamese towns and villages, the North Vietnamese forced the communist ideology on the residents. Torture and death became the grim fate of those who resisted.

The United States sent advisors, followed by ground forces over to South Vietnam. But we also sent the media. The civilian media, for perhaps the first time ever, were allowed on the battlefields, in the jungles, and in the villages during open conflict and interrogations. These journalists were able to create film, write editorials, voice opinions with limited restrictions, and were virtually unleashed on a largely naïve public. Further, these journalists had little appreciation for the larger implications of their output on the military, government, political, or social big picture. Selfishly fulfilling their personal goals of obtaining compensation for providing stories on the air and in print, they opened a window into the formerly largely unwitnessed horrors of war. They showed death and they showed it in graphic detail unlike what had been publicly shown before.

These words, pictures, and the combat footage had an impact on the American psyche. After seeing real blood, combat fatigue, our soldiers dismembered, villages shot to hell, and ultimately seeing death, the public strongly reacted with, "Stop the madness!" They spoke out in disagreement towards America's alliance with this helpless nation, South Vietnam. "*It's not our war,*" was their mantra. Hmm, as if our previous campaigns on French and English soils were *our* war. The European campaign certainly was NOT our war. It was their war. We joined their fight and made it our own. Remember now, that America's involvement in the European theater of World War II was not because of direct German aggression; unlike the Japanese's unprovoked bombing at Pearl Harbor forced us into the Pacific campaign. We, on the other hand provoked the Germans by sending arms and advisors to Western Europe. In order to cut the support lines, the Germans sunk many of our merchant marine vessels. The point is that it was not *our* war initially. We were merely supplying, and I dare say helping, our allies.

Some argued that we became directly involved in Europe in 1941 to stop Nazi aggression but the aggression began in 1937. So why did it take us four years to get involved, and if aggression was the argument for involvement, wasn't the communist aggression then a reason for us to become involved in Southeast Asia? Some arguments took the platform that human atrocities toward Jews, gypsies and homosexuals were reason for involvement, but gross human atrocities were also taking place in Indonesia, South Vietnam and Cambodia. The question then stands, why the sudden patriotism of involvement in Europe and not in Asia? The truth of the matter is that we became involved in 1941 because of British and French interests, our justification for involvement falling within the parameters of the League of Nations. We became militarily involved in 1962 because of our Asian interests, our involvement, this time falling within the parameters of the United Nations. Was our "Joe Public," back in the 1960s and 1970s, thinking rationally, or rather ethnocentrically, in criticizing our support in Vietnam?

"*So many of our boys are dying.*" Hmm, how many of our boys died in the two World wars fought on another nation's soil, no less? Hmm, why now, all of a sudden, should we not assist this nation? Is it because the Vietnamese look so different to white Americans while the Europeans looked like they could be Annie May and Uncle Frank? Is it because white America has ancestral links to Europe?

OK, so our spineless politicians here in the States, being concerned about their political futures, listened to their ethnocentric constituents protesting our involvement. The general opinion from those unfortunately very ignorant protestors was once again, "It's not our war." This opinion was being vocalized, of course, while not knowing, or giving a crap about our nation's foreign interests and how those interests affected their lives and their futures; while also not giving a crap about our reputation as a country and as a viable ally. They seemed to be unaware or uncaring about the human atrocities being perpetuated. Only a very powerful nation would be able to stop this. They did not consider the fact that an ideology like this, if given the chance to germinate, could infect, and may destroy the very fabric of our privileged existence.

It also did not help that Congress conducted their business in half-truths while haphazardly trying to satisfy public opinion. Yet, they still lobbied for continued involvement. The result of this two-faced approach was that military funding was cut, yet the soldiers remained deployed, (which basically meant that their asses were left swinging in the breeze.) This lack of funding meant there was little air support, low rations, ammunition shortages, faulty equipment and of course, low morale. This all became the catalyst for anger, and marked the beginning of tactical and operational failures by our forces. More and more of our soldiers died senselessly. Angry and disillusioned young soldiers retaliated and took their frustrations out on Asian civilians. Yet, it was the military's fault for all of this? Hmm.

Let's try another scenario; one in which America had public support as well as public ignorance. Again, World War II's European campaign becomes the defining example.

There is another side to consider in all of this. It is the side of the "haves" and the "have-nots." Unfortunately, the privileged have always taken advantage of the poor, the weak, and/or the ones less able to defend themselves. To defend and validate this point we could take at look in antiquity to the Egyptians and the Israelites; the Crown and her subjects; the immigrated Europeans and the Native Americans; the Anglos and the kidnapped Africans. This first-world mentality of superiority, arrogance, and intolerance was unmasked yet again in the jungles of Southeast Asia. Americans had little to no respect for the Vietnamese and Cambodian citizens.

So whose fault is it here? It's certainly not the fault of the Cambodians and the Vietnamese for being residents of a third-world nation, or for looking and acting different than most Americans. It may not even be the fault of the soldiers serving their tours in Asia, because aren't they just victims of their upbringing? It may not be the fault of parents and the media because aren't they just mirrors of society? So is it society's fault as a whole? But aren't societal views products of history and cultural traditions? So, given the unavoidable nature of humans and their tendency to form "sectors" in America, does this justify blatant disregard of another's humanity? Or should human beings have an innate sense of kindness that supposedly transcends race and economics?

Yes, many atrocities took place in Southeast Asia. But many seemingly impulsive military decisions, which appeared as slaughters to the American public, actually saved many American lives. How could the American public fully understand or justify this when they were fed only partial information and sensationalized fabrications? Can war ever be honorable? Can the mayhem be excused as a means to freedom and victory or, in taking that posture, are we succumbing to selfish complacency?

Regardless, Americans screamed "shame," and eventually we pulled out militarily with our heads held low.

After the fall of Saigon, now called Ho Chi Mihn city, close to a million Vietnamese civilians were forced from their homes and led out into the countryside to build Mihn's agrarian society. Hundreds of thousands perished during this transition, families were destroyed, personal liberties were lost, and America's reputation as a viable and effective ally was compromised.

It's not our war. Isn't that another way of saying it's not our business? The holocaust; was that, too, not our war/our business? Apartheid; was that, too, not our war/our business? What about the mental and physical torture of Afghani women? Is that not our war/our business? See the point yet? Selective involvement? Hypocrisy? Hmm.

So the question begs asking, would we have been successful in Southeast Asia if the public remained ignorant? In remaining ignorant, would we have allowed the military to effectively conduct their campaign? Can Americans be selectively informed, yet be effectively silenced? And should they be?

Atrocities do occur. Abuse of power in the military is rampant. We can all agree that politicians, officers, and the assailants should be held accountable and responsible, and that well-funded investigations must dig deep for the truth. Remember, though, that in war, lives are at stake, communities are in imminent danger of annihilation and genocide is not uncommon. Political futures and religious ideology are all threatened. If a country, a fundamentalist organization, or an extremist can obtain information that will protect their citizens, their soldiers, and move them closer to victory, how far can an interrogation go in order to obtain this crucial information? We label these actions as "cruel" treatment and "torture" but are we privy to what crucial information interrogations may produce or how many lives may be spared using intel obtained by these methods?

Most civilians seem to confuse rules of imprisonment with rules of interrogation, all the while screaming about human rights violations across the board. Logically, once a soldier or combatant is captured and has no useful information, they need just to be detained so as not to return to the fight. Back in the day, countries/regions took the phrase, "so as not to return to the fight," to the extreme. They took it to mean, take no prisoners; in other words, they killed all their captives. It makes cruel sense, but sense none-the-less. They (those who surrendered,) would *never* return to the fight. In this way, psychological warfare was employed by sending the message of, "this too, may happen to you". The Geneva Convention Articles were drafted to address this and many other issues. OK, once captured, a soldier should be kept alive and healthy. When you stop and think about it, harsh and unpleasant conditions actually are great impetus for soldiers to do their duty as soldiers and not treat capture as a pleasing alternative. Going overboard, the country or organization inflicting this is being down-right mean and in noncompliance with the Articles. Depending on the severity, they may be labeled as barbaric or sadistic, and the international community will condemn them for such actions.

Interrogations are another story. Before lumping the two into one, hear me out, please. War or any armed conflict is harsh; it is unpleasant; it is hell, and that is not just a cliché. It has fatal risks. Soldiers are trained to complete their mission, even if that means surrendering their life. According to military intelligence, secret operations have the most impact, and, purposely, there are limited amounts of people who will be trusted with that information. They will conceal that information at all human cost. Therefore, secrets are not divulged readily. The Third Geneva Convention forbids subjecting POWs to "cruel treatment and torture, outrages upon personal dignity and humiliating treatment." They further define *torture* as "any act that inflicts severe pain or suffering, physical or mental." First, many of those terms are subjective. What may be dismissible rhetoric to one may be mentally painful to another. A head slap or loud sounds may inflict severe pain on a migraine sufferer yet this treatment may not be as severe for one who is not. Second, if we "let them be" (captives that are knowledgeable of vital information) seriously, how else can we obtain information from them? Ask them over and over again? Say "please" several times? Absurd! Third, not all captives in time of war, unrest, military occupation, or civil disobedience are protected under the Articles of the Geneva Convention. For example, unlawful combatants are not covered, but are they not still human and therefore should have protection rights? Who determines who qualifies as unlawful combatants? Are beatings, humiliation, sleep and food deprivation, shock treatments, mind games, truth serum, and dismemberment necessary or even justified?

Interrogation atrocities, in the form of manipulating and pressuring desired statements, happen here in the states in many law enforcement departments and correctional institutions for far less vital intel. The stories are brutal, filled with flesh being cut, bones being broken, joints being popped, bodies being pounded to a bloody pulp, threats on family members, deprivation of medical care, food tampering, food deprivation, and solitary confinement. How do you really view these acts called *torture*? Is it the same? When does torture become necessary? Are you sure where you stand on human rights violation issues? Is there a different posture you take when military and civilian issues are in question? Face it, we secretly condone "by any means necessary" when it's closer to home or when the consequences are in our face, real and have a name. Most Americans cheer TV and movie heroes. Come on, you know the script. The clock is ticking, the villain will not disclose the combination that can diffuse the bomb in the elementary school basement. The impatient hero shoots the villain in the knee to get him to talk. The combination numbers roll off the villain's tongue and the elementary school is saved from the disastrous explosion. The climactic moment is when the children come bursting through the school's front door into the arms of worried, absolutely incensed parents. The hero is praised for getting the villain to talk; not charged with human rights violations. Justified?

In the late 1930's and early 1940's, German aggression was largely successful because their cause was popular. Hitler's regime fed the public dynamic propaganda, which fueled the fires of economic and social fears; the primary target of this propaganda being Arian civilians. Hitler easily amassed the support of his country. They gave him money; they gave him resources and, with great pride, even gave him their children.

Is that what America needs; to initiate mass propaganda? Can we, as Americans, be militarily successful if the public turns a blind eye and, with reservations, remains patriotic to the cause?

Are our bellies hungry for nothing else but the dramatic? Why can't we see the forest through those few unattractive trees? War is real and it is hell. Terrorism is real and it is here. Soldiers are real and they obey orders or people die. Will we become weakened as a nation with our open door policy, and with open disclosure of the atrocities, abuse and illegalities of war? Should obedience and discipline be beaten into us? Finally, and there is no getting around this question, would military reform help or hinder?

It seems that many military decisions are now products of civilian opinion. Lawmakers are frightened of losing privileges that come with elected office. The truth is, we cannot help or change certain public opinions, nor can we curb their fears, prejudices, greed, and possibly unfettered conclusions. We cannot fully educate the public or reveal sensitive matters to them. They are uninformed and hence dangerous if given a listening ear. Government does have an obligation to police the activities of the military, but please be aware that public opinion is creeping into the equation and influencing decisions made. Government officials need to be fully abreast of the battlefield situation, hey need to be firm and true to the objectives, and be fully aware of the threats and consequences of defeat. Limit the input of the public, who again, refuse to look at or do not have the ability see the big picture. Letting them, the public, "in" may cause the downfall of the misunderstood institution that protects us and protects our way of life. Should the civilian courts have a say in military training and the means to establish discipline? Hmm, we'll get to that.

Aside from the question of public opinion, the age and mentality of the average soldier poses other challenges with training. I believe we can agree that many of our youth today lack reverence and respect for their parents, elders, or any authority figure. Parents are not as active in the raising of their children as in years past. Traditional disciplinary and punishment methods are viewed as abuse. A child's rudeness is excused as the child being "expressive." Close supervision is interpreted as smothering. Anything even remotely described as quality time has long been gone. Parents today typically prefer the path of least resistance; wanting to be liked by their children rather than respected. That is what contributes to the personalities of young adults today. By the time the drill sergeant gets them, s/he needs to break through the stubbornness, laziness, immaturity, arrogance and ME mentality in order to mold the perfect soldier. I guess what I am getting at is that civilians as a whole today are harder to "break" than ever before.

At this point I feel a need to continue with extreme caution and somewhat mixed feelings because I am confused, even on where I stand, on the many issues I am about to address. I cannot condone rape, excessive physical abuse, mental tortures, nor can I encourage suicide or murder. But, without clairvoyance, I feel no one can predict what sort of military we would have without the powerful inducement of these horrors. With extreme scare tactics like these, mishaps and abuse of power are bound to occur. But the reality of their occurrence is what pulls the rope taut. *"My God, they're bound to kill me if I don't get up. Pvt. Davis got the shit kicked out of her yesterday when she did not complete this run. I have to complete it or else…"* This may sound cold, but it is reality. In life, I suppose, to get an outstanding result, one needs an outstanding reward. Ironically, the opposite extreme is also true in that, to get an outstanding result, one may have to instill an enormity of consequential fear. To break a civilian, the Army puts the fear of the Almighty into them.

After Basic Training, or "Boot," this, once-civilian, does not just act as a soldier but is a soldier through and through. Few actually do not make it through Boot. But you, the reader, do not hear much about those slackers. They are just rotated back through; some are locked up in the stockade because of discipline problems. Most pass "Boot" on the first go, though, make no mistake. You see, they frighten and or shame you into doing stuff you would not normally do which makes you perform better than you normally would perform. So there you are, a soldier, in the best shape of your life, sporting one hell of a tan, knowing a whole bunch of cadences. There, my dear reader, is the misconception. Yes, you have all of that, but you are also brainwashed to follow orders no matter what they are, so long as they come from your superior NCO (Non-Commission Officers) or CO (Commissioned Officers).

There is another point here, and that point is, you are trained to kill. Those are not just words. Stop and think about that. **You are trained to kill.** When ordered, you **must** kill. Many civilians have concealed weapons permits or are trained in the martial arts. I guess in technical terms they are trained to kill because they have the means to kill. But *must* they kill upon someone else's directive? No. A soldier must kill when **told** to kill. What do you think it would take for you to kill? What would it take for you to obey without question? This is no joke or part time gig. It is in-your-face real. As real as a fucking heart attack. Your supervisors need to know that you will follow orders and they will *train* you accordingly.

For discussion's sake, I will simplify the obligation and duties of a United States Army soldier. A soldier does his/her duty to the best of their ability. "I am an American, fighting in the forces which guard my country and my way of life. I am prepared to give my life in its defense." These words were beaten into us from day one. They are the first of the general orders of our Code of Conduct. There is zero tolerance for insubordination, debate, personal thought or discussion. Decisions come from those in office or from the Commander and Chief himself. "They" make a decision of armed conflict and those under them, like the commanding officers, are trained to strategize the implementation of a successful mission. Once developed, the plan is executed by individuals under the authority of the commanding officers. In reality, the plan is carried out by individuals expendable for the sake of victory.

The Army divisional breakdown goes as follows: Corp, Division, Brigade, Battalion, Company, Platoon, Squad, and the Troop (the single soldier.) Orders typically come down the pipe, for example: 1) Drive the communist out of South Vietnam. 2) Use ground and air forces to drive the Viet Cong past the 17th parallel. 3) The 114th Brigade will defend the Lo Sung region. 4) Echo Company of the 2nd Battalion will defend the southwest ridge. 5) Third platoon will hump their way though to Mei Lu search, destroy and prevent the flank. 6) 1st squad will go on a night recon before the 2nd and 3rd moves in. What I am getting at is that the "order" the foot soldier receives is a part of the big picture and not just an idea pulled from someone's rectum that morning. If that southwest ridge falls, the 114th Brigade may lose the whole Lo Sung region, where, let's say, a major LZ (Landing zone) has been set up for supplies. The specifics, logistics, and legalities are not necessary for the ears of the foot soldier. What s/he must do is follow the orders explicitly so the team and mission do not fall apart. Whether they may think another plan would be more effective, whether they think the casualty count will be high, (or if they be included in this casualty count,) whether they are scared, whether they are tired or have the sniffles, have cramps, or the worst yeast infection of their lives, they must obey.

So how does an individual suddenly stop asking questions? How does one obey? How does one risk and sacrifice the entity of their very being? Again, think about that. A decision which is not your own has been made and you must be prepared to die for it. I can possibly understand blind love being a deciding factor, or even revenge or honor, but hell, that's your decision. It is personal. But, just because "they" said so? I think not.

Shall we open our eyes and look about us? The common denominator of elite forces like the French Legion, Rangers, Royal Navy, Navy Seal team, and Green Beret is discipline. It's not just their special warfare training. They are the most intensely, disciplined and obedient units in the world. Their training definitely weeds out those who can not physically, mentally, or emotionally meet the challenges. Those who can't measure-up, die or are rejected, and are pumped like raw sewage back into the civilian population. Suffice to say, then, that a strong team demands obedience. So we are still at the same question. How, then, can you suddenly become obedient?

OK, you see those traffic controllers "being all that they can be," sporting a smile and having the time of their lives. Most of you who have not served say, "Oh, it's not that bad. It kind of looks lik fun." THEY ARE ACTING! They may even be professional actors and actresses. That is not the attitude in the real military. I hope you truly understand that. Buried behind those smiles are robots programmed to perform exactly what they are told. They are programmed to, without question, perform acts that they may have questioned before the "process."

Example: Orders are sent to an aviator to "down" an aircraft that has strayed into our airspace. Now, the average civilian may want confirmation for themselves before they shoot what may be a passenger plane filled with friendlies. But that's not your job. Your job is to shoot. So you do. You are expected to do it. Why? Because, those are your orders. *They* said so. There's no room for a gunner to sit back and ask why. If you question, you are a liability to yourself, to your unit, to the military and to your country. Could you do that? If not, you are not, nor could you be, a soldier.

In the Army the drill sergeants have eight weeks to break a recruit; eight weeks to tear down every inch of their individuality and build this recruit into a soldier; a robot that follows orders without a blink of the eye. They will take a civilian and drive them to the point where they are no longer proud of whom they see in the mirror. There is no place in the military for individual admiration; self love; self-preservation. *One is none, two is one.* Meaning, as an individual you are nothing but in a group you become one effective, highly motivated unit. There are only two loves in the Army; your unit and your country.

Boot camp is a crash course in harnessing killer instincts. It is about building a team, physical conditioning, and unfortunately about brainwashing. The fear of consequences and the sense of duty breeds obedience. Consequences in Boot could range from shame, to humiliation; from extra duty, to sleep deprivation; from bruises, to confinement; from missing teeth, to permanent scaring; from harassment, to rape; from a dishonorable discharge, to death.

Another issue is the role of women in the military. Although many experiences are similar to those of a young man, a woman's experience may not entirely parallel. There still exists the prejudices that stem from the military being a man's haven. In prejudice I am referring to the assumption of physical inferiority of women and the prevailing perception that women are unable to cope with the horrors of war. Only 52 percent of jobs in Army are open to women, only 59 percent in the Navy and 20 percent in the Marine Corp. The Air Force comes in at a beautiful 97 percent. Although no law prohibits women from serving in combat in the Army, service policy restricts women roles by Title 10, USC 3012 of the Department of Defense. This gives the Secretary of the Army authority to determine personnel policy. The Secretary of the Army has developed policies that exclude women from routine engagement in "direct combat." "Direct combat," where the term "close contact," is used by other military branches, is defined as:

> Engaging an enemy with individual or crew served weapons while being exposed to direct enemy fire in high probability of direct contact with enemy's personnel and a substantial risk of capture. Direct combat takes place while closing with the enemy by fire

maneuver or shock effect in order to destroy or capture or while repelling assault by fire, close combat or counter attack.

Outside of the United States, five NATO nations have no combat exclusion laws or policies: Canada, Denmark, Luxembourg, Norway and Portugal. Women in Canada and Denmark are trained as fighter pilots. Ironically, and hypocritically, the U.S. Air Force trains Danish female fighter pilots but will not train U.S. Air Force female pilots to fly fighter aircrafts. Examples of Army Military Occupation Specialties (MOS) that are off limits to women are Infantry, Combat Engineer, Field Artillery, Special Forces, Armor and Aviation Operations. Combat support jobs, which are open to women include; Medical Specialist, Supply Services, Intelligence, and Communications. Then there are clerical, law enforcement, administrative services, electronic maintenance, public affairs and tech jobs.

In Boot, all but the Military Police are trained the same. The MPs are separated from the rest of us for a joint Basic and law enforcement training. Boot trains a civilian to be a soldier despite their MOS and is some what gender-blind. The difference, at least in the Army, is only in the Physical Fitness Test (number of pushups, sit-ups, time in the 2-mile run, etc.) The marksmanship, weapons drills, miles in the forced marches, military conduct and field performance are similar. It's not until Advanced Individual Training (AIT) that the soldier learns his or her job. For example, as a Medical Specialist (Medic), I learned to basically patch up soldiers. Medics are the first line of defense against combat death. We need to be trained in such a way that we are crawling forward as the infantry is pulling back. They are doing their duty on the field of battle or in the MASH unit rather than making an offensive charge or hiding in a hole crying. You also need to establish trust amongst your fellow soldiers that you can be depended on when the familiar call of 'MEDIC' is uttered. But being a medic has its hazards. Yes, I learned weapon-offensives, but as a Medic, in accordance with the Geneva Convention, I cannot display any aggressive action and may not use lethal force. I only resort to arms in defense of the wounded and sick. Here is the joke, if you want to call it that; the Articles of the Geneva Convention also state that medical personnel are not to be targets. So, if all goes well, we aren't shot at and we can go about our job tending to the wounded. However, as shown in South East Asia, the Red-Cross armband and ambulance markings only served as a bull's eye. The Viet Cong targeted medical personnel, especially as a part of their psychological warfare. You see, if the medic is killed, the morale of the soldiers also takes a blow. Anyway the point is, despite my medic's oath, or despite anyone else's primary job, we were first trained as field soldiers similar to infantry. A soldier, whether they are a man or woman, needs to project a certain confidence in their physical abilities. Their buddies depend on them and they, in turn, depend and trust their buddies. Simply put, we needed to be tough as hell.

But therein lies the paradox. If a woman holds on to her femininity and genteel demeanor, thus falling short of the toughness required of the Army, she is at high risk for sexual molestation or unnecessary humiliation by those who wish to prove her fragility. If a woman makes the grade and excels in all aspects of her training, she is labeled and targeted as a lesbian and that witch-hunt will be her constant shadow. Inflated and dramatic opinions are formed and insinuations made. Then, a dishonorable discharge ensues. If not yet brought to court, this highly motivated soldier will be verbally abused and challenged excessively. She may even be ostracized by her own gender, other females not wanting to be guilty by association, you see. As many of my comrades did, I found myself rejecting any sort of friendship. Tough male soldiers can have close buddies with which they run and party. A tough female soldier's buddies are soon viewed as possible lovers. So we, as female soldiers, tried to prove that we are competent soldiers but were damned if we are too convincing.

"Oh, look at that sweetie. She can't do shit...figures though, she's just a little woman. How did she get in here anyway? I would kill to bang her. Yeah buddy, papa is in the house. She wants it. You know that's why she's here."

or,

"Shit man, look at her go. Goddamn, she's fast. Did she make all hits? I heard, man, that she can do like 50 pushups. Yeah? Oh, must be a dyke."

God, with all this pressure was it any wonder that it was a crazy hell-hole of suicides, rapes, AWOL, fights, witch hunts, loneliness, helplessness, constipation, nausea, profanity, and manipulation? But was it JUSTIFIED?

I cannot answer that.

2

The Political Question

I grew up in the 70's in Kingston Jamaica. We migrated from this *tropical paradise* in 1978. That same year the People's National Party (PNP), the party in power, was headed by Prime Minister Michael Manley. His political platform was based on an ideology called Democratic Socialism. He politicked and preached of an egalitarian system of social and economic equality which leant itself with great similarity to Marxist theories; government control of industry, medicine and education. Desperate and impoverished Jamaicans interpreted this dreamer's philosophy literally and assumed the posture that they had the right, responsibility and obligation to bridge the gap between the wealthy and them, the victims. Further fueling the fall from grace, in the eyes of the American government, was his overt alliance with Cuba's dictator, Fidel Castro.

The opposition, the Jamaica Labor Party (JLP), was headed by Edward Seaga. His political platform was more directed towards unionization of industry, capitalist business, corporate expansion and the financial growth of the working class. Seaga made no secret about his alliance with Richard Nixon, Gerald Ford, James Carter, and the former CIA director. Proponents saw his JLP platform initiative as a path to prosperity and getting people back to work. Opponents, on the other hand, feared and predicted natural resource and labor exploitations. Whatever the case, the last thing America needed was a communist sympathizer, Prime Minister Manley, in office in Jamaica.

The country I now call my own was neck deep in the destabilization of Jamaica. The objective for overthrow was not a dramatic removal of

Prime Minister Manley by kidnapping or assassination, but rather the target was the country's economy. You see, fall-out from a stagflation, is social unrest and an intolerable move towards change. To hold office during a time of severe recession is political suicide. Once the economy spirals out of control, the Gross National Product (GNP) plummets, foreign businesses leave, the wealthy panic and transfer their funds to overseas accounts. In addition, local businesses declare bankruptcy, the country sees mass unemployment, there is inflation on goods and services, availability of foreign products becomes scarce, austerity sets in, and poverty follows. Unfortunately then, destitute and impoverished citizens resort to crime, and renegade groups form to attempt coups in the desperate desire to improve. There is actually no need for obvious external intervention if the economy crashes.

After Manley won re-election in 1977, the United States encouraged the Group of 10 (G-10)—industrial countries that managed the International Monetary System (IMS)—to limit their importation of Jamaican goods and to over-inflate their exports. Despite their gross mismanagement of loans from the International Monetary Fund (IMF), Jamaica was still allowed to borrow, which plunged the little island into serious debt. Jamaica, with declining exports and an increased need for imports and a huge national budget deficit, had to devalue the currency and deflate the entire economy to re-establish a competitive trade position. This was akin to political suicide for Michael Manley.

In addition, between 1976 and 1978, a tide of high powered weapons flowed like bloody currency from the U.S. into the hands of the JLP's political gunmen. Violence escalated to an alarming intensity. Wealthy homes were burglarized. Children of wealthy families were targeted for kidnapping in hopes of obtaining ransom. Wives and daughter of the wealthy were being raped in order to create humiliation and shame amongst the pompous aristocrats. The violence was so rampant that it drove 9% of Jamaica's population to run to Canada, England or the United States. The lines were drawn through Kingston with West Kingston being the PNP stronghold and East Kingston being a JLP stronghold. Within this time period we as a family, being strong and known PNP affiliates, never ventured into East Kingston. There were numerous assignations and mortal statements made in the name of party affiliations.

Large automatic weapons were not foreign to me. I saw the police, military personnel, political gunmen, and gang leaders carrying them freely through the streets of Kingston. This arrogance and posturing represented power and control. On a smaller scale, my father also carried a pistol on him at all times to protect himself and his family. We were viewed as a part of Jamaica's aristocracy. Under strict supervision and with it unloaded, I was allowed to hold his weapon. I watched Dad load and unload it. I watched as he cleaned and stored it. I watched when he drew it in anticipation of trouble. "Honey?......Kids?......It's OK, I'll take care of it." And out came the gun. Oh, how I wanted one, too. It symbolized power in my naïve eyes. I saw it, though, as a source of defense rather than a weapon of aggression.

The smell of a rotting corpse was also not foreign to me. Mom and Dad protected my innocent eyes from seeing its origin but the smell was so distinct and was so intense that there was no protection from that. The corpses were typically victims of political gang warfare or that of an unknown indigent. It's not like here in the States where the police and/or medical examiner's/coroner's office is immediately notified and the spectacle removed. Oh no. The police were elsewhere dodging bullets, quieting a riot or plumb hiding; not wanting to get involved. You see, most likely the killing was an assassination, hence a political statement. In removing the body, similar to removing a blockade, it would be seen by the opposition and taken as a counter-statement; quite an insulting one at that. Snipers and/or opposition informants may be lurking. The deceased's family may have to be the ones to pick up the body and that in itself was a dangerous move because they may be followed and may even be targets.

The protective measures at home were viewed as normal to me at the time. It was not until I came here in the States that it became evident that not everyone lived on alert. It was not uncommon for our driver, and later my parents, to take different routes home to insure we were not followed. We had armed security guards patrolling the property. We had five trained guard dogs. We had iron bars (in Jamaica called grills) on every window and door with panic alarms situated in different parts of the house. Upon driving into the property, we were crunched in the car and there was a quickened step from car to the side door. That kind of behavior and lifestyle was that of the "privileged." You must have clout, money, or assets; something that someone else wanted desperately. Therefore, as processed in my young mind, it was an honor to live in fear. The more security measures taken, the more the family had.

Although not allowed to participate, the primary topics of conversation around the house were centered on the political climate of the country, police brutality, non unionized sweatshops, secondary school favoritism and the latest strike (whether it be sanitation workers, truck and bus drivers, the electric company, the water company, school teachers, cemetery laborers, bank tellers, sugar cane cutters, dock loaders, or the only broadcast company.) It just went from bad to worse. Funny, it didn't matter if you were rich or poor, once the water company went on strike…, water was cut off for EVERYONE. No shower; no sprinklers; no boiled rice; no boiled or mashed potatoes; no drinking water. The bucket below the roof drain and the chlorinated water in the pool would have to suffice in the flushing of the toilets. Back then drinking water was not sold in jugs like here in the States. Being wealthy only meant more candles when the electricity cut off. Oh also, without electricity, the security systems did not work, so there was a heightened state of alertness.

In an effort to save the country from economic collapse, Prime Minister Manley and his ministers installed a safety net to keep the money on the island. Importations were limited in an attempt to make

Jamaica, as a country, more self-reliant. Foreign businesses were expelled and citizens were forbidden to take monetary resources out of the country. To insure the success of this plan, spies were employed to eradicate and flush out the CIA operatives and halt all attempts at money transfers. However, as you might expect, many ingenious tactics came out of this mud paddy. People, like my parents, devised schemes for getting their money out. But the government also had elaborate schemes, and unfortunately, severe punishments were used on individuals who were caught. The spies would tip off officials when families were seen packing for a migratory move. Small planes would fly over residential areas since fences would block the view of those on foot. At the harbor, mattresses were torn apart. Holes were drilled into furniture. Toys, tools and appliances were disassembled. At school, children were interrogated away from their parents. In the city, bank accounts would be checked and some were frozen. At the airport, families and friends were questioned and suitcases were ripped.

My brother, sister and I were told only a few days before our furniture started to disappear. You see, we never saw the moving truck although I do remember seeing the packers. The truck was not parked outside the house but was parked elsewhere where the spies would not be able to tip off the freight and dock officials. In the dead of night and occasionally in the mornings some boxes would be transported in smaller vehicles to the rendezvous point. As for our hard earned, honestly made money, let's just say Mom and Dad were real artists of deception. I am hesitant to go into detail lest I foil another desperate family's attempt in trickery. We fled Jamaica with enough money for a new start in United States.

Soon before we left, though, I felt the danger closing in. No longer were we allowed to play in the yard. We needed to stay indoors. Suspicious men would be seen at the gate. Our gardener was suddenly let go. The chauffeur was fired. Both could no longer be trusted. Mom kept a watchful eye on the maids and soon took over all the cooking responsibilities. Then one of our guard dogs was poisoned. Yep, it was time to leave. With only a limited amount of suitcases in hand, cameras strung around our necks, big fluffy hats on, and conversation staged around seeing Mickey and Minnie Mouse, we boarded Air Jamaica and departed for Fort Wayne, Indiana by way of Miami, Florida.

OK, so after the ass of rhetoric is beaten to its pathetic knees, the question stands, "When a country is on the brink of economic collapse, are political tactics of this magnitude justified?" In the aftermath, the 1980's in Jamaica saw a cesspool pool of corruption. There was the birth of the infamous "posses," as the gangs came to be called, from the womb of Kingston's dilapidated and diseased endometrium. There was an influx of drugs, especially crack cocaine. There were numerous seizures of property. Banks without insurance just closed their doors. Heart-wrenching devaluation of the dollar made purchasing foreign goods almost impossible and nonessential products like silk, disposable diapers, beef, automotive parts, feminine products, electronics, jewelry, leather goods, and cereal were widely unavailable. There was also an increase in illiteracy. Education became too expensive, teachers migrated, and schools closed their doors. The government allocated their limited funds to the immediate, (tourism) instead of the future (children.) Basically, the systemic destabilization of the country was successful. Manley was eventually voted out of office and the threat of communist alliance was severed. Jamaica lay in ruins.

This sort of "success" story was foreshadowed in the nation of Chile where, through America's intervention, a similar, and largely forgotten, destabilization situation manifested. Should America take on this international responsibility? Is homeland security reason enough? In his attempt to save his beloved country, were Manley's tactics justified? Was the social backlash of autocratic self reliance justified? For those who deserted and economically raped Jamaica, were we justified?

3

Interest

Jamaica's military was made up of the Jamaican Defense Force (JDF) and the Jamaica Constabulary Force (JCF), but neither really had the strength or the resources to put up a fight against external aggression. The military was more for maintaining order if and when the police no longer could. Sometimes they were used for legitimate civil unrest, but frequently Prime Minister Manley would declare a State of Emergency just so he could have access to the JDF and JCF in order to strike at the opposition. He would deploy the tanks and troops into East Kingston, create havoc, and then gloat in his show of force. Of course the next day, another one of his ministers would be found dead in West Kingston or a Political Science Professor with affiliation to the PNP would be dramatically kidnapped from his classroom at University of the West Indies, or another mansion would be torched. My God, it just went from bad to worse.

The military base in Kingston, called "camp," was located directly behind the public library. When I should have been concentrating on my studies, I would be mesmerized watching the soldiers train. My best friend at the time, Elaine, was the daughter of Brigadier General Green. So when I visited her, that place would be "camp." How cool was that? Imagine, surrounded by hundreds of soldiers who despite their probable silent objection, HAD to entertain us. In driving around with Elaine, her father and the chauffeur, every soldier (commissioned and non-commissioned) had to salute the passing vehicle. On foot, forget about it, people left and right were snapping to attention. On several occasions the pilots took us up in the helicopter. I even had a chance to visit, what were in my opinion at the time, the condemned and pathetics in the stockade. About two hundred yards from the General's house were the security barracks where about sixteen soldiers bunked. These were the guys that pulled guard in shifts around the mansion. Although told not to go there, Elaine and I used to sneak back and hang out with the fellows. They did not violate us in any way, but they certainly didn't tone down their swearing or carrying-on when we were around. They smoked tobacco and weed, joked around, wrestled, and ragged on each other. All in fun. They allowed us to hold their unloaded rifles and made fun of the fact that we were not strong enough to hold it up. "Such little princesses. Alright pretty girls, run back to General now. Remember this is our secret. Remember to give me a call when y'all grow up."

On one of my visits to "camp," I witnessed a sight that ultimately changed my life. On this particular day, as usual, I watched as the new recruits jogged by in cadence. They carried their M-14 rifles on guard (in front of them with affixed bayonets), belted out the hoo rahs; they were all in step, wearing those loud heavy boots, dust stirring with every pounding step, like puffs of smoke. In the mist of all of this toughness, I saw a woman. I knew it was a woman because, well, there was some bouncing going on between her neck and her belt. I had assumed that the military was only for men. I was overwhelmed with all kinds of emotions. I felt proud that women were represented in such a hard core team. I was worried for her that maybe she didn't belong there and was trying to be in disguise. I was frightened and worried that my parents would lock me up if I told them I, too, wanted to enlist in the JDF, carry a gun and wear combat boots. Anyway, that's all she wrote. My mind was made up. "When I grow up, I want to be a soldier."

The USA in 1978 was exploding with excitement. The roads were wide, smooth, and animal and garbage free. Buildings were so tall. TV was in color. Lights just seemed brighter. The music was different. Foods had no taste. The cars were so long and wide. Back East, Studio

54 was opening its doors and New York was becoming the ultimate velvet rope party capital. Down South, race riots were still raging but now instead of the actual integration of schools the riot centered on police brutality and forced busing in order to integrate schools. The Mariel boat lifts (April 1980–Sept. 1980), sparking the modern Cuban invasion, had not arrived as yet, so Miami was still economically in the hands of Anglos, although, there definitely was a Latin flare around town. Out West, the sexual revolution was at its height with San Francisco being the mecca for all gays needing a sense of security, a sense of acceptance and a place for sexual expression. The bathhouses were still open and frequented by the more promiscuous sect of the gay community. The coffee shops were filled with colorful, yet starving artists. Gloria Gaynor, Abba, Diana Ross, Peaches and Herb and the Bee Gees were the all sensation. Lavern and Shirley, Fantasy Island, Love Boat, Eight is Enough and CHIPs were on the tube. Leif Garrett, Eric Estrada, Andy Gibb and Scott Baio were plastered on the bedroom walls of most young girls. Grease had just opened and Saturday Night Fever opened the year before. Disco was the craze. A peanut farmer from Georgia was the leader of this new land and the elected president before him was a confirmed abuse of power needing to resign before impeachment.

We fled a country on the brink of economic collapse and came to a country riddled with racial discrimination. Discrimination also existed in Jamaica but it was more so social discrimination than racial. There were many very well-respected, extremely dark individuals holding top position. It was a rude awakening here in the States. Even with money, education, manners and morals, parents would still forbid their kids to play with us, realtors would show us homes only in certain areas, and many of the private schools would not accept our entrance application. We were excluded from community sporting and children's events, got the stares, and were generally avoided at church, were called derogatory names, and were even threatened.

Mom and Dad did manage to enroll us at St Jude Catholic Preparatory school. I believe they became aggressive after initially taking a passive, less confrontational approach. As the story goes, they threatened to sue the school and personally sue the Principal. We, as innocent kids, came onto the scene without fear or even hesitation, and really did not understand the aversion and tension we created just by our presence. Finally, my parents who tried so hard to shield us from the hatefulness of many Americans, sat us down and told us delicately that, "They" (the whites) not only see us as different but inferior, and may even see us as threats. They, the whites, think we are less than them. They are just looking and waiting like vultures for us to make a mistake. Therefore, we must not give them that 'opportunity.' We will show them that we are better human beings than they, and when they refuse to recognize their own mediocrity, that will be their shame. When they are shown that it's they who are the threat, they who are mean, they who are unkind, that will be their shame. If and when they lower themselves to illegalities, we will fight them in their courts." That was the driving force for Dad at work, Mom around town and the neighborhood and us kids at school.

Within a few months, Dad became his company's top salesman in Indiana. Mom kept all family matters in well check; the finances, the home, our spiritual growth, etc. In reference to school, she made sure our uniforms were crisp and clean every morning. She made sure we did our homework, that we were prepared for the next day's lessons, and made sure we understood the lessons previous. Mom always dressed her best to go to the store, to drop us off or come pick us up at school. Her hair, clothes and makeup were flawless. She was always polite to everyone she saw, although she never waited for them to return a greeting. I do not think she really cared. Mom just did what was right with a smile. Our marks at school were great. It was not as if we were brilliant children but it was that our studies were emphasized at home. Homework and extra "Mom-given assignments" had to be done and checked before any TV or playing outside. Another scholastic advantage was that the Jamaican school system was far ahead of the American one. So material received at St. Jude like mathematics, grammar, geography, basic sciences and music were already covered a year or two before in Jamaica. The school allowed Wayne, my brother, on the football team but did not allow him to play at the games, until one evening, the coach put him in toward the end of the game. Wayne was the wide receiver. The quarterback threw him a short pass, he caught it and ran for a touchdown. Imagine that? This was the first time Wayne touched the ball in a real game. His speed was so impressive that the fans, despite the objection from the other player's parents, pressured the coach to give him more playing time. Nicole (my sister) and I tried out for the basketball team but were not chosen. I thought we were two of the better players but I guess the coach saw different. Disappointed, yes we were, but it forced us to concentrate more on the objective activities, as I like to call them; activities that were not left to opinion, prejudice or otherwise. Activities like our studies. We tried to get the top grade on exams and assignments. We tried to have the best penmanship. We tried to always have our hand up first to answer questions in class, although we were seldom asked to answer the questions. So there it was; our first year in the States. We did not have many friends. We became suspicious, distrusting and disenchanted with what we saw as a lack of basic humanity of those around us. Yes, there were many changes upon our arrival to America. What did not change for me though, was my attraction to the military.

Daddy subscribed to Reader's Digest and between the pages of one of the books I found a post card to send away for information about the United States Army. Secretly, I filled it out. I didn't like school anyway, so why not, right? Why not join the Army? I plugged in the information asked for, like date of birth and so forth. I entered 12/07/68. A few weeks later, I received a booklet and a very polite letter reading, "Thank you for your interest in the U.S. Army. Please contact us in another nine years." Of course, my parents found my rejection letter belly grabbing hilarious. Fueling the flame was that I presented them with the unread letter thinking it was my acceptance letter. I cried for what seemed like hours. "Why not?" I thought. "I could make a darn good soldier. And I am sure by now, I can hold up the rifle. I could learn. I am tough. Well, fine. I'll show them. I'll prove I am fit to be a soldier." So off I went into life's abyss showing the world, and then some, that I was an unrecognized, unappreciated soldier.

Determined and fanatical as I was, I started feverishly collecting those plastic soldiers, and tank and weaponry figurines. I mutilated every magazine I could get my hands on, cutting out pictures of fighter jets, guns and battle scenes. Where my sister had heartthrobs on her bedroom wall, there I was ornamenting my wall with icons of war. On my eleventh birthday Mom humored my obsession by baking an appropriate cake. She made it with two bread pan molds, then shaping them like two "1s." She then arranged my figurines in a trench-war-fare-like manner. Loved it! Tanks were on top of the trench, the flame throwers behind them, some infantry guys still in the trenches and some along side the flame throwers, some prone, some standing. How cool was that?

It was now Kalamazoo, Michigan and to back track a bit, Dad being the top salesman in Indiana was sent to this remote area of Kalamazoo; low in sales. Hmm, was that a promotion, was that a business strategy, or was he embarrassing his white co-workers with his achievements. This time around, my parents enrolled us in public school where the discriminatory challenges, like what we faced back at private school in Indiana, seemed to diminish. Perhaps Kalamazoo was more progressive or perhaps more liberal. Maybe times were just changing. Whatever the case, I could now pursue athletics unencumbered. Nicole concentrated more on her studies and social interactions. Wayne, well he was a star on the track and on the football field.

A few years after moving to Michigan, I was introduced to the saxophone but it was not until high school in Ohio that marching band came into play in my path to enlistment. Same scenario.

Dad once again was top salesman, so they transferred him and the family to Lima, Ohio; a less productive area in sales. High school marching band in Ohio had the precursor elements I was looking for. It had the discipline, the calisthenics, the cadences, the marching in step, the uniform and the respect. Unfortunately for me it had the slip-ups that would ultimately follow me into the Army. Maybe I tried too hard or maybe I was just a bona fide goof ball, but boy did I make some memorable fuck-ups. The first one wasn't all that bad. There we were at Summer Band Camp practicing for the upcoming football season. Training us in discipline, the order from the band director was to stand at attention without moving until he instructed us to go to parade rest. Instruments were held firmly in front of us, our elbows out, chest up, head forward, feet together. There wouldn't have been a problem except for the damn bee that landed on my upper lip. Knowing what the director's orders were but also weighing the cosmetic implications and painful eventuality of a sting, I made the impulsive decision to go against orders and break attention in order to remove this uninvited guest. In a sea of stillness came an insane flailing of arms and instrument. From a distance I guess it looked like I lost my mind and despite my desperate attempts, I was not given the opportunity to explain my madness. I was just told to run a couple of laps around the field. Accepting my punishment I ran them in full stride figuratively beating myself up for reacting and breaking attention. Already thinking like a soldier, I was lambasting myself. Whatever the situation was, I shouldn't have disobeyed orders.

The next, more memorable slip-up was Homecoming Game. Of course it had to be Homecoming Game. Nicole was Drum Major (Field Commander) that year. Being Field Commander you led the band onto the field, you saluted the fans, you directed and conducted the band through the performance, and then you marched them off the field. We were so proud of her. Oh, on the by and by, Nicole was the first black Field Commander in Shawnee High School's 65 year history. Anyway, back to the half time show. It was a signature stamp how Shawnee Marching Band entered the field. Nicole or those who came before her, would do their impressive salute, clap their hands four times, yell, "Band, Atten-tion." The band of about 150 musicians would, on the count of one, put one knee and the hand holding our instrument up, and scream "Shawn..." On the count of two would snap to full attention, instruments grasped with both hands and scream "Nee." For years this had been a tradition. Alumni, students and fans would roar. On this particular performance; Homecoming no less, our director wanted to surprise those in the stands by doing a silent atten-tion (it's all about the effect.) At the last minute, on the sidelines, he passed the word that we would have this damn silent atten-tion. I, being preoccupied with something probably quite trivial, heard the order then forgot the order. We all lined up and went to parade rest; instruments to our sides, feet apart, head bowed. The announcer over the field loud speaker announced, "For our half time show I would like to present the Ohio High School state champions, the Shawnee Marching Band led by Nicole Forbes and Beth Wannamaker." I heard the four claps and the "Band, Atten-tion." My knee went up, instru-ment went up and I screamed "SHAWN." Instantly remembering the change and of course only hearing my voice, I impulsively said, with approximately the same projection, "SHIT." So what the entire field, stands and parking lot heard was a lone loud "SHAWN-SHIT." Standing there at attention wanting to be sucked into the field, hearing the crowed roaring with laughter, I glanced over to my sister. Her head just dropped. She recognized the voice. She knew it was her dear little sister fucking up again. The game was known as the shawnshit game. Yep. I got it. Running laps, loading the bus, staying after band practice, running laps, unloading the bus, and running more laps until my senior year. Unfortunately, these foul ups would follow me straight into the Army a few years later.

While in high school I heard of the military academies; honorable institutions like the Army's West Point, the Navy's Annapolis, and the Air Force's Colorado Springs. This was quite the concept. Imagine, going to University, being military and at the end being commissioned as an officer. Fabulous! After my decision was made, I started positioning myself for acceptance. There were many requirements and conditions; some within my power like scholastic and athletic standings, but others were not like being nominated by a congressman or senator. From ninth grade onwards I started racking up the varsity letters, kept my grades high, became visible in honor clubs and organization, volunteered at local hospitals and convalescent homes and scored relatively high on my ACT. In addition, I passed my physical aptitude and medical tests. During the later part of my junior year I submitted my application for nomination. I believed I stood an excellent chance being a top scholar, being female and most importantly, being black. You have to remember that affirmative action, although not called that as yet, was being recognized at the Federal level. Fair, racially sound decisions had to be made or discriminatory suspicions would ensue.

That summer, my dreams fell apart. Dad had a racially motivated falling out with his employer of 18 years. Soon after, he accepted another position with another company but this position would constitute relocation back to Jamaica. Nicole was entering Ohio State University that Fall and Wayne and I were finishing up high school so, not wanting to pull us out of the American education system, the decision was made for Mom to stay here in the States. The catch to the plan was that we as a family, minus Nicole, would move to Miami, Florida so Dad could economically fly back and forth. The move pulled me out of the nomination district, and the timing of the move disqualified me to apply for nomination down in Miami. Badda-bing, badda-boom.

In weighing my options of the possibility of applying the following year, my chances now looked grim. Miami was more competitive both in the Academy and for congressional applications. My new Miami teachers would not know me so their letters of recommendation would be lacking. Coaches in Miami also didn't know me, and I would be a year older than the ideal acceptance age. In my disappointment I sought the advice from local recruiters. Friends and classmates at the time were harping on the Air Force being the branch for nerds, the Navy being the branch for the soft, the Army being the branch for the intellectually challenged, and the Marines being the branch for the masochist. I decided to join the nerds. The Air Force recruiter ill informed me that I could become an officer "in no time" by enlisting. But first I would need to take a test called the ASVAB (Armed Services Vocational Aptitude Battery.) My memory does not serve for me to remember what I got, but it was pretty high; high enough to qualify me for Military Intelligence, Military Police, Nuclear Technician, Medic and such. Military Intelligence sounded great; sounded cool.

My scores were forwarded via computer to the recruiter's office. Keeping my appointment, I met with the recruiter to discuss my career options. Without checking his computer he started encouraging me to consider these low scoring careers. A little confused I asked about Military Intelligence, Medic and so forth. The pompous Jackass actually said with half a crack smile, "Well, you need a pretty high score on ASVAB for those you mentioned." I told him my score and it was then that he checked his computer for confirmation. Oh, hmm, suddenly a change in career categories. Now insulted, I just got up and left his office. His assumptions pissed me off. As I was walking back to my car, Sergeant Brown of the Army waved at me through his office window. I smiled and thought, "hell no, the Army is for idiots, I ain't going out like that." He waved again and signaled for me to come in and talk. I hesitated first then, figured I'd give him/them a listening ear. Immediately, without asking if I sat the exam or what my score was, he began enticing me with the jobs I actually wanted. Unfortunately, I was still not a United States citizen; a basic requirement for intelligence and law enforcement work. I ended up choosing Medical Specialist 91-Alpha; now called Health Care Specialist 91-Whiskey. Within a few weeks I was signing a contract and taking my Army medical physical. Both Mom and Dad reluctantly signed the necessary release forms and on December 27th, 1985, twenty days after my seventeenth birthday, I took the oath to defend my country (USA) against all enemies foreign and domestic.

4

On My Way

Parents were not allowed at the MEPS (Military Entrance Processing Station.) Dad flew up from Jamaica just to see me off. Mom with teary eyes helped me pack. That Thursday morning I waved good bye to my parents standing there in the driveway. As Sergeant Brown and I pulled away Mom buried her head into Dad's chest sobbing. I, too, was crying. It was not just leaving my parents that forced my tears, but leaving everything and everyone I knew, leaving behind adolescence and its security, entering into this unknown abyss, doubting my decision, the "now-what?" and the "oh-crap what have I done?" Sergeant Brown looked at me and said, "Oh for God sakes, buck up. You are soon to be a soldier. Buck up now."

Before we arrived at MEPS, I kept going over in my mind if I brought everything: my drivers license, my social security card, my phone numbers, my contact lens saline solution, my Jerry Curl activator, my tooth brush, my sun block, my Bengay. Funny, although I packed all of those items, only the first two followed me to Boot camp, but we'll get to that. At MEPS before the front door, Sergeant Brown gave me a cold pat hug and a thumbs-up. "Here you are Nadine. Good luck. Bye now." There it went. Truly, everyone I knew was gone. I stood there for a while holding my suitcase looking at the door wondering what to do. Eventually, I walked through the doors and entered a waiting room of mean looking, loud, obnoxious men. Completely intimidated I asked this larger than life uniformed guy behind the front desk if this is where I should be. He just said, "Yes," and walked away. So I turned back around and wandered to the back of the room to wait, for I do not know what. He returned, looking annoyed at something and yelled "SIT DOWN." Everyone scrambled for a chair like it was musical chairs and began planting it. Of course being so petrified by the order, I just looked around like a lost crazy woman. Every chair I reached for was snatched up by one of the mean men in the room. I eventually planted it on my suitcase so I would not be the last one standing. He called us one-by-one into a room where another officer gave us two meal tickets, a packet containing our military file and orders, and a plane ticket voucher to our Boot Camp destination. Some of the men were going to Fort Benning, Georgia; Fort Chambell, Kentucky; Fort Bragg, North Carolina; or Fort Hood, Texas. My destination was Fort McClellan, Alabama. Before we all left MEPS a Priest came in full dress habit, said a few prayers, and handed us all New Testament Bibles. Oh, that really made things lighter. What? LAST RIGHTS?

In accordance with my packet orders, I was to fly into Atlanta, Georgia (somehow) and take the "Alabama Limousine" to Fort McClellan, Alabama by 12:00 midnight. If I was not there, I would be AWOL hence could be arrested and incarcerated for five years. There were no instructions on how to use the vouchers, which airline to take, departure times, maps, nothing. I, who was not bold, enough as yet, was not used to confidently asking questions at places like airports. Mom or Dad always did that. I always stayed in the back and reaped the benefits of someone else's assertiveness. Now I had to fend for myself or quite frankly, be locked up. Yikes. I eventually, timidly, asked the right people the right questions and got myself booked on a flight to Atlanta.

As I sat in the gate waiting area, many thoughts ran through my mind. One was back to the consequences if I couldn't get a flight. My gosh, I guess I would just make my way up to Canada, find a job and live in hiding for the rest of my life. Other thoughts were of the future. "What will I see and experience in the Army that will change my life? Will it actually change my life? How will people see me? How will I see myself? How will I act? Who will I meet? Will there be a war? How much of the world will I see? How will I look in Army greens?" Anyway, my flight was sometime before noon, maybe around 11:00 am, or so, and I got into Atlanta in the early afternoon. There at Atlanta's airport I saw many uniformed soldiers, I guess from Fort Benning, Fort Gordon, Fort McPherson or Fort Stewart. I thought, "Soon I will be one of them." There was something though about their eyes that struck me. They had a modest, shy, yet harsh look about them, as if they were bruised. Their eyes were piercing; angry and scared, all wrapped up in one look. It was so strikingly obvious that I just sat for a while observing each of them as they caught my eye. I now, after my experience "in," understand what I saw several years ago at Atlanta International Airport. Maybe, you, the reader, will have a clearer understanding after reading my story.

Anyway, I used one of my meal tickets in the airport before I was off on my next adventure to find the "Alabama Limousine." With my humble experience with vehicles, I approached the parked stretch limos with dapper men holding large cards. I looked for my name on their cards and not seeing my name I asked one of the gentlemen, "Which one of you guys is taking me to Alabama?" Confused, he asked for clarity. I said, "The Alabama limousine is suppose to take me to Fort McClellan. So when do we leave?" He laughed and pointed to a modest bus about 200 meters away called The Alabama Limousine. Oops.

So I walked over to the bus. It did not have a driver but the door was open. Apparently, some of the bus's passengers saw my blunder, so upon entering the bus, the laughing and the jeering started. "Yo-Yo high society! Decided to join us, huh?" "She thinks she's the shit? Welcome to hell, sweetie." I was mortified. All these unfamiliar mocking faces just looking at me. I guess I really didn't expect to see Mom sitting in the front seat of the bus, but I really didn't expect such awful looking impolite people; poking fun at little old me, no less. No one to help fight this battle if they all physical ganged up on me and ripped my fragile 110-pound body to shreds. The women on the bus were all older than I and sat more toward the back. The men also looked older than I did, and they sat more in the front. I decided to sit by myself somewhere in the middle. There was a scent of stale perspiration in the air and a certain mood of unsupervised chaos. After about three hours of unbreathable stuffiness, vulgarity and sheer boredom, I asked the guy in the next seat, "Excuse me, sir do you know what time we are suppose to leave?" He replied, "Sir? What the…?", with knitted brows. "Do I look like a fucking tour guide? I don't fucking know……dyke," as he turned back to looking out the window at nothing. How rude, I thought. And what the heck is a *dyke*? I obviously was living quite a sheltered life compared to these heathens.

Alright then. I picked up my suitcase deciding to go for a walk, to use my second meal ticket, get into some air conditioning and use the restroom. Since this decision came right after the tour guide comment, the guy pursued his attack on me as I was leaving. "Ah, I hurt her feelings. Look, she's going to go cry now. She'll never make it. She'll wash out before she even gets to Boot." Needless to say, when I came back, he started in on me again. "Look boys!! Ah shit. Looks like I have money for y' all." "Why," I thought, "is this guy after me? I just asked him a simple question and I believed I was polite about it. Now he is casting bets that I would go AWOL, calling me dyke (whatever that means) and cursing at me". When I thought the worst of the afternoon was over, the belching contest started. The women started it with hopes of outbelching the men. Great! That was all I needed. I had just gotten a sandwich and now I have to deal with a bus filled with gastrointestinal fumes.

At about 1700 hours, not more than 10 minutes after I got back to the bus, the driver, Satan or a thief got into the driver's seat, closed the door, started the bus and began exiting the airport grounds. He did not introduce himself nor did he take roll. He just took off. What if I decided to make a few calls home, or stroll around, or had problems in the bathroom? I would have had to hitch-hike to base; in another state; and get there before 12 midnight or have five years to think about it.

"My gosh man. What the hell have I gotten myself into?" No one else seemed alarmed so I just settled in for a long bus ride.

There was a nip in the air and I remember looking out at the rocky cliff-like highlands of west Georgia. My eyes closed with a sense of peacefulness. It would be long time until I felt that peacefulness again.

The bus came to a sudden stop. Still half-sleeping, my eyes eventually focused on a guard gate with Military Police posted. The gate pole lifted then lowered behind us. Immediately my heart started racing like I have never felt it race before. "Yikes, what have I done. I am here, can't reset this game." The bus turned right and left then left again and right; went in what seemed like a deceptively purposeful route of evasion. In actuality it really wasn't but everything seemed so dramatic. Voices became muffled as I strained to absorb my new home. There were no aluminum barracks as I had seen on the sitcom, *Gomer Pile* or pitched tents like in the movie, *Galipoli*. There were one-and two-story, regular brick and mortar modern buildings. There were no mounted machine guns on jeeps or rolling tanks. What I did notice off the cuff was that, even in the night, I could see the grounds were very well manicured.

The bus stopped and Satan venomly hissed his first words for the evening…"Get Off." I was not anxious to get off but I sure the heck was not staying on. He pointed at a side door of the adjacent building behind which our welcoming party of three waited. My fellow comrades giggled their way off the bus and through the door of the office. Immediately the welcoming party jumped to their feet and called us all 'pitiful fucks.' I thought, "Nah, hang on, now. It's them, not me. I have been a victim of association." They then hollered, "If you all think this is summer camp, you are sadly mistaken." Another said, "Send this batch back. They belong in a zoo not in my Army." Can you believe I got excited? Excited to maybe be going back home. Go figure. For most of my life up to that point all I wanted was to join the military and in no less than a day, I was ready to go home. It was my first taste of helplessness and irrational consequences. See, no one was around to hold my hand through this new process. If I got it wrong, or right for that matter, there would be, like, these major consequences. I didn't insult or confront the bus passengers, yet I was verbally attacked. I was polite to someone in asking a legitimate question, yet he in turn returned with such an aggressive vile tongue. Now these idiots I came in with have caused me to be grouped into a category of miserable, oh no, *pitiful* fucks." Yep, wanted to go home.

One guy in the bus group snickered at the welcoming's party seriousness. Before we knew it, the NCO (Non-Commissioned Officer) climbed over the counter and slammed the guy against the wall; all in about three seconds. Hell, man, he came over the counter, not around. Normal people go around desks and counters, right? His forearm was jammed between the recruit's jawbone and his throat. He may even have started to lift the guy off his feet. His body and face were so close to the recruit I thought if he just puckered, they would have kissed. His body was so close the recruit couldn't squeeze his hand between them to free his throat. This smart aleck was called all sorts of filthy names; words and expletives I had never heard before. Things I thought that were off limits just flew from his mouth. He attacked the guy's mother, his body odor, his hair cut, his upbringing, his breath, and his lack of strength to save his own pathetic life. The NCO called the recruit a sissy because between the yes-sirs and no-sirs, his voice started cracking. That, in itself, made the NCO even more annoyed because, as I found out later, you never call a NCO *Sir* or *Ma'am*. That was reserved for the commanding officers, who, according to them, were paper pushers. He then asked him the weirdest question, I thought at the time. He asked the recruit if he liked it up the ass. Hmm…*it*? What's "*it*?"

When the NCO released the recruit, he initially grasped his throat gasping for air, then grabbed his midsection and then threw up. Instinctively we all took a big step away from him; distancing ourselves from what was about to happen. Oh my Lord. You would have thought the world fell off its axis. All three of the NCOs just exploded in a mob like frenzy. "What the FUCK?" "Oh no, he did NOT..." "I am going to KILL this......" "Son of a BITCH......" "This mother fucking bitch had better..." "Let me at him." "I'll tear his mother fucking head......" I just stood there like a deer caught in headlights. They made him take off his own shirt and wipe his vomit off the floor.

The attention was then turned back to us. We were told that if we wanted to speak, sneeze, smile, fart, yawn or move, we needed to ask permission. I saw a shadow of movement to my left; a raised hand. The NCO looked at the guy and hollered, "This is no fucking Sunday School!" and ignored his attempt for attention. One woman then asked if she could speak. The NCO said "No." One by one they ran down the rules. "You may not go here. You may not go there. Never do this. Never do that. The mess hall is over here. Your sleeping quarters are over there. This building houses the infirmary. You will be here, the reception station, for five days (because of the weekend.) If you need more clothes the PX is over there, but never go there without permission. On Tuesday you will be issued your uniforms and equipment. You are still nothing, so don't try *nothing*. Don't try saluting because you don't know how. Do not try marching because you don't know how. Do not dare talk or look at a commanding officer. Do not try going to at-ease or attention because you don't know how." They then told us to one by one go behind this green curtain and dispose of any cigarettes, drugs, firearms and/or knives that we might have brought with us. No questions will be asked of the disposed items. I thought that was absolutely ridiculous. Who the hell would bring a gun to the Army or would want to risk getting high? Little did I know that in only a few weeks I would be cursing like a sailor, smoking whenever I could get away with it, using drugs whenever I could get way with it, fighting with both soldiers and drill sergeants, contemplating murder, and behaving like I had no couth. And yes, within a few days, I eventually found out what *dyke* meant and what *it* up the ass was all about, too.

It is amazing looking back on how that situation could turn such a straight laced individual as me into a completely different person. It was not as if I made an effort to fit in. I just changed.

Punishments did not make sense. Punishments without cause were learned to be expected. They just existed without reason. So a soldier becomes confused, cynical and mistrusting. To get the point across, violence was always used. No asking; no warning. If your hands were too far apart doing pushups, you got a flailing kick in your ribs. "Do them right Private." If you were out of step marching or running, you were violently yanked out of formation and thrown to the ground. "Beat your mug Private." If the boots by your bunk were not shined enough, they were thrown at you standing there at-ease. "What the fuck do you call this Private. Do them right." If you left your soft cap on indoors, they would grab the bib, pull it down almost to your eyes, swing you around a little, yank it off and smack you with it. "Pick up your cover, Private, then get your ass outside and give me fifty." If they caught you talking during chow, they would come up behind you, grab you by your collar and physically drag you out of the mess hall for "motivational" exercises. "Apparently you are not hungry. Very well......" I mean the sergeants could spot you from across the room; then make a beeline for you, knocking recruits down in the process. You just wanted to fold up and die; hoping to God they were not coming for you. If you're pretty sure it's you they are coming for, you try to pile as much of your meal in your mouth before you are grabbed up. Although we knew of the possibility of being grabbed up, it would behoove us to remain seated just so we could finish as much of our meal. Plus, also, if we were not the one they were after, and we got up from sheer guilt and avoidance of the physical aspect of the ordeal, well you were out there, too, with the observed guilty party.

Yes, punishment was excessive and for the most part unwarranted, but also we all were running on less than 5 hours sleep per night. Sleep deprivation also added to my mental dissent and newly found aggressiveness. After lights out we really didn't sleep soundly. Some of us were writing letters under a flashlight, some writing papers (*Why I like the U.S. Army/How to Stand at Attention/The Importance of Physical Training to a Soldier in the U.S. Army, etc.*) assigned as punishment, and some of us were just sniffling, trying so hard to stifle our whimpering.

Rape was rampant, especially during boot camp. So there was that added anxiety of when they would come in the night for you; if they would come for you, "Aye, (violent shake), wake up. Get your boots on, Private, and follow me." That was the same command used when they marched you away for midnight motivational exercises or newly assigned guard duty. So you never knew what was ahead that evening.

It was a helpless situation because we had absolutely no support; no guardian of our rights. Sergeants always protected their own and damn well made sure you never complained again. We could not formally file a complaint or grievance. Where would we file it? We didn't have access to a mailbox or a computer. Our calls were monitored and times assigned. No one who could make a difference would listen to us. If I asked to see a commissioned officer, the sergeants would say "no." Then I would be punished for asking. We could try and run but since we all didn't know where the exits were, it made the running alternative not very attractive. You see, everywhere an enlistee goes (the PX, the rifle range, classes, the mess hall, the parade area, PT), we are marched there by a drill sergeant or the platoon leader. You just did not see a single lonely private rooming by herself. The military police would quickly pick you up or another sergeant would take matters into his/her own hands and chase you down like a runaway slave.

Once you had come to grips with the fact that you, indeed, were alone and had no rights, you settled into obedience and submissiveness. Matter of fact, you became thankful for small favors: Only one slap instead of a series of them; the sergeants waiting for your platoon to pass by before they hammered you (allowing you to save face); permitting you to do your motivational exercises on the concrete rather than in the mud; sleeping in 'til 0500.

Many factors drove us to our wit's end. It didn't take long for me to discover, embrace, and worship my beloved splif and my pills. What I am referring to is, yes, narcotics. My preferred drug was Speed, clinically referred to as amphetamines. After a few weeks of sleep deprivation, even the screaming, ordering, spitting, pushing, slapping, threats, and shoving of the drill sergeants had little effect. I was so tired. I started making stupid mistakes like turning right when I should to turning left, sounding off at the wrong times during cadence, running into things (poles, signs, trees), forgetting to salute an officer, plumb not hearing reveille, starting off (marching) with my right instead of my left foot, falling asleep standing in formation, showing up at formation half dressed, falling asleep prone with my weapon (with live ammo) pointing down range. I became sloppy during my drills and I became more and more depressed. I started having thoughts of suicide. I even once forgot which bunk was mine. A buddy of mine, who always seemed to be on top of things, introduced me to Uppers. Soon Speed was a necessity to get the day started. Unfortunately Speed suppresses your appetite, so considering the physical demand on us, we had to keep our use in check. Another drug used was Pot. That was more on the weekend, though, to get the monkey off our back. Cocaine was too unpredictable. Heroin was not readily accessible, plus I hated needles. LSD and magic mushrooms were for idiots who definitely wanted a court martial. Ecstasy hadn't hit the streets as yet. Another rampant drug was anabolic steroids affectionately called 'Roids'. Oh, those pretty purple pills. Although I was attracted to the effects of Roids (enhanced endurance and musculature), I chose not to go that route hearing so much about "roid rage." That was the last thing I needed on top of my natural rage, compounding it with Speed and Roids. Yep, that's asking for trouble.

Well, back to the first day. Our order packets were taken from us, the idiot wiped up his vomit, sexes were split up and the men and women were led into separate barracks. The door of our new barracks flew open and we shuffled into this dark room with bunks everywhere.

The male sergeant who led us there said, "Find an empty bunk, find an empty locker and go to sleep. Wear shorts because I do not want to see or smell pussy in the morning. Good night." Good Lord, I thought, what a vulgar little man.

In the midst of the darkness I found an empty bunk and locker, and took out a pair of shorts to wear under my pastel nighty. I sheepishly laid my head down on a pillow I could not see. It smelt like bleach so that was a good sign, I guess. I covered myself with the sheet, also smelling like bleach and a very rough feeling blanket.

At about 0500, the lights came on. With eyes squinting and heart pounding, I heard a male voice hollering that we had fifteen minutes to get outside. I thought, "For the love of Christ, fifteen minutes is rather pushed. Why didn't he come in fifteen minute earlier or better yet an hour earlier to give us a little more time?" Looking around I realized that I was the only one in a nighty. The other ladies had on boxers and a T-shirt or sweats and a T-shirt. Some of them picked up on that too. They just pointed and rolled their eyes. "Looks like we may have a Private Benjamin amongst us, hee hee." I was not amused. Me, a Private Benjamin!!!! It was just one wake up call after another. I didn't know what to say any more. I didn't know what to wear anymore. I didn't know how to eat, less I be poked fun of again. Weird! I thought I was through with all of that back in high school. I was a jock with several varsity letters. I held a few karate trophies under my belt, and took pride in boasting that I was a member of the Cobras (this group of young martial artists in the neighborhood). Yeah, big deal. I was sitting there in a pastel nighty with polished nails.

The latrines (bathrooms) were to the back of the barracks. The stalls had no doors and many of the women did not have the courtesy to look the other way as you did your business. They just stood there (in a nice single filed line facing each stall) giving you the look as if to say, "I'm sure you can pee faster than that." I just lowered my head in embarrassment.

We made it outside in fifteen minutes. A total of about thirty women were in the barracks. Some had been there for a few days. Some of us were new. It was Friday morning. We newcomers who arrived on Thursday night were told that we would be there (reception station) for three working days. Therefore, we were not leaving until Tuesday. If we needed to purchase more civilian clothes, the PX (Post Exchange/ store) was available. I took advantage of that opportunity to buy some more shorts, a pair of sweats and a few more t-shirts. There was no way in hell that nighty was being worn again.

For the next few days, we were taught how to walk without sashaying, how to march in step, how to make a bunk, how to do pushups, how to turn, how to sit when eating and how to identify ranks. Little did I know at the time but these few days were invaluable. You see once a recruit reaches boot camp, it is assumed that they know these things (how to march, how to do a pushup, etc). It is there that you will be told to do them; not taught to do them. If done incorrectly, for example, marching with a strut or wiggle, you were severely punished. If you were asked to do thirty pushups and they were done incorrectly, the count would begin on the first correctly performed pushup. You would not be told what you were doing wrong. At Boot you were drilled, drilled and drilled on what was instructed on at the reception station. One of the things we were taught only in Boot, though, was how to hold and fire our weapons. Also, parade drills were only taught at Boot camp.

Our wills and life insurance matters were handled at the reception station. Our pictures were taken. We were fitted and tested for issued spectacles. Medical shots were given and it was mandatory that we sent a letter back home (with picture enclosed). Now all this time, with the exception of the initial welcome, there was a certain gentleness of tone. Even when taught how to do a push up, or a sit up, we were just shown. We didn't have to do any if we did not want to. I called home. The call was not monitored. I told Mom I was in great spirits and that it was easier than I thought.

HA…little did I know what was in store.

We watched movies in the evenings. We ate great meals during the day; taking thirty minutes or more to leisurely chew and swallow. Some of us took lazy walks around the compound after we ate. We laughed; we socialized; some of us played cards.

On Monday, the barracks cleared out. Just the six of us who came in on Thursday remained. That night, at around 2300 the door of the barracks flew open and about fifteen women shuffled in. I heard a male voice say, "Find an empty bunk, find an empty locker and go to sleep. Wear shorts because I do not want to see or smell pussy in the morning. Good night." I smile like a seasoned veteran.

5

Boot Camp First Day

On Tuesday all hell broke loose. As usual, I left the barracks with my wallet in my back jeans pocket. Unknowingly, that morning my wallet would be my only civilian possession for quite a while.

We convened after morning chow in the auditorium where we were asked to, one-by-one, approach an evaluator and do two good push-ups. The guys, I believe, had to do 8 or so. If you, as a woman, could not do two good, regulation pushups, the evaluator failed you and sent you off to pre-boot camp for a couple of weeks. There I believe they worked on your upper body strength. I had absolutely no difficulty with those measly two pushups. Matter of fact, I radiated a certain amount of arrogance when asked to do them. I am sure looking back, the evaluator must have written in my records, *"Private Forbes seems to be a show off. She may need to be humbled."* After the pushup ordeal, the guys were lead away for their hair cuts and us women were led to the Wells Fargo for forwarded cash and started on the measuring process for our uniforms. When we saw the men again they were completely bald. It was not the crew cut you may have seen on TV. Nope. Bald as bald could be. Some men gave themselves crew cuts before they arrived. They, too, were led away. All returned from the barbers with no hair. It is amazing how similar men of the same race look when they have no hair. This was all part of the breaking down process. They began removing all traces of individualism.

At the uniform depot we were asked to strip to our underwear and place our civilian garments in an assigned bag. I remember at the last minute I reached back in and grabbed my wallet. From there our heads, feet, waists, leg length, shoulders and chests were measured. This information was given to a runner to take to the next room. In the next room, piles of stuff were given us. I really do not remember the exact count but it was something to this effect. A few brown t-shirts, two summer full BDU (battle dress uniforms), two winter full BDUs, two pairs of boots, two belts, a few pairs of green socks, two soft caps, and a long duffel bag. I believe our one set of dog tags with cover was given to us at this time also. The non-commissioned officers told us to put on a T-shirt, socks, a set of summer BDU, belt, and our boots and to pack the rest. They told us also to take out one of the soft caps but for the time being, roll it up and put it in the side BDU pocket. Whenever a soldier goes indoors, the soft cap immediately comes off. When they return to the outdoors, the soft cap must always go back on the head. If something did not fit, especially the boots, to inform them immediately. Otherwise, we were told to board the bus directly outside the depot. When on the bus, a guy said that some people were packing up our lockers and storing our *shit*.

It then occurred to me that was it. What I had on my back and in my duffel bag was it. No jewelry, no address book, no tampons, no photo album, no deodorant, no Jerry Curl activator, no contacts, no perfume. I didn't even have a toothbrush. Like, what the hell?

Oh, the bus was not a bus. It was more along the lines of a cattle car with tiny slits for ventilation. No seats; just a few poles. When the cattle car was full, the driver told us to strap our duffel bags in front of us. Of course that made no sense to me but we all followed orders and strapped the forty-pound sack in front of us. We drove, stopped, turned, stopped, drove, stopped, and turned in what seemed like a circle. After a while I lost my bearings of where the reception station was to our present location. As the cattle car stopped, the metal doors would slide open and last names hollered at us by ugly men and women in sergeant hats waiting beyond the doors. Those whose names were called shuffled out and the rest of us just sighed with relief.

Finally, my name was called and I shuffled out the door, still not used to my boots, with, as you remember, a forty-pound bag strapped in front of me. So there I was, running down this trail leading to what seemed like nowhere, and looking like a pregnant woman with twins trying to run. Immediately, I was attacked. "Move it. Move it. Move it, you skinny fuck. I hate you already. Don't look at me. Move, move, move. You know why I hate you, you skinny fuck?" Out of breath (yes, already), I sheepishly asked, why? He screamed even louder, "Because you think you are something special, because you think you are better than any other pitiful fuck that's here, because you smell, because you run funny. You are nothing, you hear me private. You are nothing. And you know what else, fool?" I did not answer. I was still on the 'smell' part of his colorful answer. He said louder. "And you know what, fool?" I stopped running, raised my eyebrows, turned to him and said 'WHAT?' "Oh, it's going to be like that, huh? Come with me." Duffel bag and all, I followed him. Before I knew it I was doing push-ups with the bag now strapped to my back. He didn't give me a number. He just said down, up, down, up, down, up. Being an athlete I was knocking them out. What I should have done was to huff, puff and squeal like an old woman at ten. But no, I wanted to impress. At about twenty five (you have to remember now that the bag was on my back) I was thinking, alright, this kind of sucks. My arms started to shake and it looked like I didn't impress him one bit. Still with his down, up, down, up, shit. With back arching, neck muscle tendons popping out, teeth clenched, I tried to squeeze a few more out when an added weight was thrown on my back. Boom! I hit the turf. Then the ass-wipe stepped on me. I didn't even have time to turn my head. Nose first in the grass. I heard him say, "On your feet." I rolled over (no longer able to push myself up) in a daze, dusting the dirt and grass off my face. "Stand at-ease." He looked at me real close for about ten seconds then stepped back and said, "Say, thank you, drill sergeant." Again I raised my eyebrows as in, 'EXCUSE ME.' "Very well, beat your mug private." Although that was the first time I had heard such an expression, somehow, I knew what that meant. Yep, more pushups.

If anyone started out thinking that the boot camp experience was a joke, was comical, or was this Hollywood play act, the sergeants quickly changed that line of thinking. They drove you to tears. They drove you to screaming. They subjected you to so much physical pain and discomfort. You became so fatigued that you wish you would just pass out. But you don't. That alone took the silly grins off our faces. Since everyone had his or her own breaking point, the harassment was individualized. For example, maybe someone else may not have minded being called skinny or being told that they smelled, but that elicited a reaction from me. Now, I did not mind if they called my mother names. I knew she was a wonderful person and no one could get my goat with trash talking. Someone else would lash out and, of course, get beaten down. Someone else would get raving mad. The Achilles heel, I tell you, was the key. They throw so many insults at you; they run you into the ground until they get THE reaction.

A few phrases were commonly heard on company grounds. "The most common was, "I can't take it no more." (Yes, double negative, but, whatever). After a while, "Army" was not uttered without "fucking" preceding it. Like. I hate *this fucking Army*. Can't wait to get out of this *fucking Army*. Why did I sign up for this *fucking Army?*" Our vocabulary slowly changed. Bathrooms became latrines. Beds became bunks. Guns, oh guns were never called guns. They were weapons or your M-16-A-1 rifles. Stuff became gear. Your pistol, when holstered, was your side-arm. Friends became buddies. Cap became cover. Helmet was steel pot. The hospital or clinics became the infirmary. Sleep became Zees. Cigarettes became smokes. If you didn't know someone's name, they were then called soldier. "Pick it up there soldier." If you got a glimpse of their rank, then it was "Let's go, private." Few soldiers knew my first name. Matter of fact, hearing it reminded me of my previous life. You see, because of the disparity; the absolute dramatic difference in existence, life before Boot indeed seemed like a different life all-together. So friends called each other by their last names, versions of their last names or an affectionate description of their personality. For example soon I was known to my buddies as Forbsy. Private Lonue who grew up in LA with nannies was known as Hollywood.

Oops, off on a tangent again. Let's get back to first day of Boot. So there I was in the grass doing pushups. It didn't take me long to figure out what I needed to say before I died from fatigue in that God-forsaken place. Exhausted, I was told to get to my feet. I got up with an apparently detectable "attitude." Hell, I was called names, asked to thank my humilator, reacted to the humiliation and then was punished some more. Of course man, I will have attitude. Now, how did this all begin? Was it because I ran funny or was it because I, according to him, smelled? Oh yeah, it was that "thank you" shit. He looked me square in the eyes and said, "Do you have something to say to me." Reluctantly, I started to say, "Thank you" but before I could get the "TH" out, he roared at me telling me that if I even thought or dared to challenge his authority, he would lock me up in the stockade so fast. Now say "thank you drill sergeant for strengthening my mind and my body. Feel free to do so at any time." Oh hell, now the thank you had been extended to a full-blown complex sentence. I did. I said what I had to say. He returned with "…Didn't mean it, Private, beat your mug."

Great start, I'd say. Once I finally got to join my fellow scared recruits, I realized that most of them were also getting the first day initiation. Women were crying, hacking, falling down, crawling, shaking; just looking completely overwhelmed. Some of them genuinely looked like they were running in circles; not knowing what to do, where to go, what to say, who to look at, who not to look at. The common theme was, "what the hell did I do?" or "is this for real?"

Once all dusty and sweaty, we were led with tongues of fire into the barracks, told to put our gear down on the nearest bunk. "Your bunk mate is your buddy. You will be firing live ammo over her head and she over yours. Get to know your buddy." Before I had a chance to meet my new buddy, Pvt. Fisher, we were ordered back outside.

Canvas covered trucks came and transported us to the Supply Warehouse. There we were issued various items like a gas mask, poncho, flashlight, rucksack, pistol belt, suspenders, ammo pouches, steel pot, steel pot liners, shovel and earplugs. The supply sergeant, a mean looking fellow, apparently told the platoon to check all items for flaws before leaving the warehouse, but while he was giving these specific instructions, I was, again, doing pushups in a nearby field. Get this. My crime was looking and smiling at a passing jeep. The jeep was cool as hell, and the driver, well, was cool-looking too. According to my Drill Serg, my mind was not on task. It needed re-motivating. Anyway, I did not get the chance to check my gear but I remember the Supply Sergeant saying, as we were leaving, "If I see any of you pitiful fucks back here, you'll wish you were dead." He got the nod of approval from our drill sergeants and off we were again.

Yep, needless to say, old Forbsy was back. You see, it rained that afternoon and we had to put on our newly acquired ponchos. Mine, of course had this beautiful rip in the front so large as to flap proudly in the wind. I had to be transported privately back for a new poncho. First, the supply sergeant was bawled out for giving me defective gear. Then my drill sergeant jumped in the jeep that brought me and left. The man left me with the pissed off demon from the fires of hell. You know I would have been quite content with my torn poncho, but no, I had to be thrown to Lucifer. The forty-five minutes of pushups, scissor cuts, and jumping jacks were not the worst of my punishment. He was so vile and cruel. His words, his tone, the stomping, the grabbing of his crotch, the cursing, the spiting; that's what scared the crap out of me; not to mention the facial expressions of death and madness. Ever been spit at, where the saliva lands on you?...let's say, your face? Well, it is not pleasant. It feels first like a jell splat, then it just slivers down where gravity sends it. You feel the point of contact and you feel the entire travel route until it dries. After it dries then the crust line is still felt until you have a chance to wipe or scrape it off. It is also damn rude and disgusting. He also kicked dirt at me as I did those crazy motivational exercises. The dirt thing (everything is relative) I could handle. At least it was not bodily fluid. Coming to think of it, even when someone is pissed off at you, there is still that sense of civility where they spit at your shoes or spit in your direction. But the facial contact is just out of this world degrading.

OK, once I got back to the barracks I had to do twenty pushups before entering; a new rule specially drafted for me whenever I entered the barracks. There the platoon was enjoying brief down-time where they were packing away their gear and making up their bunks. Pvt. Fisher took one look at me and said, "Damn, what happened to you?" At that point, for the first time since arriving, I really wanted to cry. Things were happening so fast and so intensely that I could not really grasp what was happening. Now, as the pace slowed, it occurred to me how unhappy I was and how hopeless the situation was. I held back the tears, shook my head, scratched my brow and softly asked what else I needed to check in my gear. She replied that I had to definitely check the gas mask for filters. Yep, without fail, I had no filters. That's all she wrote. Couldn't hold them back. Busted out crying. "Why me? I can't take it no more." There was no way in hell I was going to mention this missing item. The supply sergeant, no doubt, would put me in the infirmary. If need be, I would just have to hold my breath if a nuclear warhead was to fall on the barracks. I just wanted to go home.

Later in the afternoon, we were given a list of necessary items to buy at the PX. Items included things like a comb, toothbrush, toothpaste, tampons/pads, soap, Battalion PT shorts and T-shirts, towels and washcloths. At the checkout counter the sergeants stood with vigilance checking our stuff. Now, a few unlisted luxury items were granted like foot powder, lip balm, aspirins, laxatives, and nail clippers. Most luxury items were sent back. Some in the platoon tried to buy styling gel, sent back. Some tried skin lotion, sent back. Some tried chewing gum; sent back. I tried to get away with razors, those too were sent back.

"Hairy legs here I come." There in the convenience store I struck up a conversation with four male soldiers. I noticed their boots were super worn. They were in graduation week, their 8th week, and pretty excited about finishing Boot. Giving me some survival advice, they warned me to just do what I was told and not make any waves; not to show off; just keep a low profile; life would be easier. But from across the store, my Drill sergeant spotted me talking with them, came over, and screamed at me for some kind of breach of conduct. Apparently female and male soldiers were not allowed to "fraternize" and I was "fraternizing." So there was the irony of it all, because of those who were warning me to keep a low profile, I was now **not** keeping a low profile but rather being bawled out in front of all the patrons of this convenience store.

Couldn't do anything right.

There at the PX we were given the option to see the barbers. It wasn't mandatory but they frightened us so much with the, "Don't let me catch a strand of hair below your collar," bullshit, that most of us opted to cut off our hair. Considering the pace of the first day I should have slept well that night, huh?

Nope.

6

Typical Day

The first day of Basic Training will always be remembered; I can't honestly say, *fondly*. But truly, it will be remembered. The days and weeks to follow flew by at a feverish pace; I made new friends, I got in a whole bunch of trouble, I started smoking, I became dependent on drugs, I overcame my shyness, I laughed a little, I cried a lot, I gained twelve pounds of muscle, I turned two shades darker, I saw women break into emotional pieces, I saw soldiers physically beaten to a pulp, and I developed pleasure in bloodying slackers. Most of all, I learned how to be a soldier; how to use my weapons, my fists, my strength to save my life, save my fellow soldier's life, and save the democracy of this country. I learned how to operate within a unit and to overlook the injustice of the process.

In 1985 I was an Army recruit of the Second Battalion-Alpha Company-Third Platoon, stationed at Fort McClellan, Alabama. There were forty-four soldiers in my platoon and four platoons in Alpha Company. All of Alpha Company-Second Battalion trained together and graduated together, but we slept and socialized as separate Platoons. Although the entire company had to be in formation, class, drill, chow, and range together, we formed, sat and marched as separate blocks. Eventually, it became a kind of competition between the platoons. Whether it be which one of the platoon leaders was the better fighter, fastest runner, sharpest shooter, roughest looking or which of the platoons scored the highest at PT or at the range. Ironically, the Army was training us to work as a unit, yet actively encouraged rivalry amongst the platoons. Go figure. I became caught up majorly in this, because being squad leader and later platoon leader, I was pressured into fighting the battles for my platoon or pressured into being the top athlete. If I looked bad, the platoon looked bad.

The mornings began at 0400 with the lights blasting on, whistles blowing and some kind of profanity shouted at us. "Get up and get your mother-fucking asses in formation in 25 minutes. Move, move, move!" If the sergeant came fully into the barracks instead of just to the door, a soldier closest to the door of entry would scream "At-ease front and center." It was always comical seeing us all trying to wake up, some of us jumping off the top bunks, and getting to at-ease in a half sleep state. Most of us slept in our PT shorts and T-shirt so it didn't take long to get it together and get out into formation. Since we only had 15 minutes between PT and morning chow, we used time between wakeup and PT to start working on shaping up the barracks for inspection, doing jobs like cleaning the latrine and mopping the floors. Our bunks had to be precisely tucked with proper tautness and all angles cornered. Our belongings, in and out of the locker, had to be arranged and rolled precisely to standard. T-shirt rolled to the length of a dollar bill, socks rolled and lined, uniforms hung in specific order, equipment and rucksack ready to go. At 0430 the entire company was called to attention. In a formation parade situation, if memory serves, the Company Commander's commands were echoed by the Drill Sergeants, by the Platoon leaders, and then by the Squad leaders. "Company,---------Platoon-----------Squad-----------Atten-tion. Right,-----------R-i-g-h-t, R----------i--------g-------h--------t-----------Face. Forward, f-o-r-w-a-r-d, f---o---r---w---a---r---d............March." We would be marched down to the PT field where the fun began. Jumping jacks, windmills, pushups, sit-ups, and scissor-cuts would be performed under tongue of fire. Movements would be done to count (for example, when doing push-ups, on one, we would go down, two we would push up, three we would go back down.) The drill sergeants would count:

"1–2–3–"

and we would chant, "One!"

Then they again, 1–2–3–
And we, "Two!"
1–2–3–
"Three!"

So, if you worked it out, we were doing twice as many as *our* count. When we, the recruits, reached, let's say, 30. We would have actually done 60. They would not give us a terminal number. They would just count. Eight drill sergeants would move in and around the PT lines screaming at those who couldn't hack it. If someone couldn't handle the exercises, those soldiers would make it longer and harder for the rest of us, because the count wouldn't continue until the slacker got back in unison with the rest of us.

After about 30 minutes worth of the exercises we would be again called to attention and led away double-time for the two-mile run. The run was never just two miles. If a slacker falls out of the run, the pack (now individual platoons) would be led maybe 30 yards ahead of the falling soul, turn around, circle 30 yards behind the slacker, and come back around for her. If she did not get back into formation this would continue until she did it on her own or one of us physically pulled her sorry-ass back in. Of course whoever got her would basically have to drag her, at pace, for the rest of the run. So the choice was, continue going in circles or drag someone along. Needless to say, a slacker really got it from all of us once we got back to the barracks. Upon return to the barracks at around 0545, those of us, like me, would have to do our accumulated demerit pushups before entering the barracks door. Remember I accumulated 20 the first day. Short of a shower, we quickly tended to our personal hygiene, changed into our BDUs, fin-ished the last touches on the barracks, and got back out into formation by 0600; off to morning chow.

I have absolutely no complaints about Army food, whether it is breakfast (morning chow,) lunch (afternoon chow) or dinner (evening chow.) The only problem I had was with the time allotted to eat. Give or take a minute, we had seven minutes to put down our food. The first few days I just made real bad selections on food and drink. There was so much to choose from. All of it looking and smelling great. There were eggs, bacon, honey-marinated ham, pancakes, waffles, hash browns, tator tots, French toast, fresh fruit, yogurt, coffee, tea, cereals (five different kinds,) milk, juices (three different kinds,) corned beef hash. My God. You name it, they had it. At first I chose the coffee (to stay awake), the pancakes and cereal (for carbs,) the eggs and ham (for my protein), and fruit (for instant energy). Yes, I have a healthy appetite. But that didn't last long because at seven minutes into the meal, when the drill sergeant screamed, "On your feet. Get your sorry-asses out in formation." You had to have nothing left on your tray except empty cartons and plates. I couldn't do it. Hell, my coffee wasn't even drinkable until five minutes into the meal. Pancakes took chewing time. Ham needed to be cut. Fruit required chewing. Cereal also took pouring time. Not cool. I was out doing motivational exercises and going hungry the first week until I learned the ART OF EATING. First, never choose anything that requires pouring, cutting, chewing or cooling. Extra serving of scrambled eggs, four cartoons of milk, a couple spoon-servings of hash browns and a glass of juice was the breakfast of champions. The eggs were taken in first, then the milk and the juice were gulped in the next few minutes, and lastly the hash browns were piled into the mouth and into expandable cheeks in the last few minutes. The last bit of chewing and swallowing was done on the way to the tray station and running out into formation. By the time I lined up, breakfast was done. As for afternoon and evening chow, the same applied. I only asked for stuff I didn't have to chew like meat sauce, stew, rice, and mashed potatoes.

After chow we would get the results of the barracks inspection and either be marched over to the classroom building, marched across base to the rifle/pistol range, or marched over to the battle training field.

The classroom curriculum consisted of military history, roles and responsibilities, ranks, code of conduct in time of peace, in war, and as prisoner of war, articles of the Geneva Convention, weapons engineering (US and foreign weaponry,) basic first aid, basic auto mechanics, and map/compass reading. There was absolutely no talking, whispering, clearing of throats or getting up without permission. Whenever an instructor would enter the huge classroom (seating the whole company,) we, on command, would snap to attention then to at-ease. At-ease is a funny command. There is nothing at ease about at-ease. You still can't move or speak. The only difference between being at attention and being at ease is instead of having your feet together with your arms to the side, your forearms and hands are behind your back and your feet are separated. Anyway, the instructor would follow with "Take-your-seats." Within two seconds we had to be seated, chairs adjusted, head forward, feet flat on the floor, backs straight, pencils in writing hand and both forearms on the desk. No more sound (moving of chairs, coughing, rustling of paper) was allowed. What we could do though, without permission, was drink water from our canteens after class had begun. (reach, open, drink, close, re-holster.) If we were so sleepy that we felt we were plumb going to fall out or do the head-nod-jerk, we could raise our hands and ask one of the roaming sergeants if we could stand (at at-ease) in the back of the classroom. Ever fallen asleep standing up? You would think you would fall back or fall forward, huh? Nope. Your knees actually buckle first. Then, you go straight down. By the time your mind registers that your equilibrium has suddenly changed (rapid descent,) most likely you would have already collapsed.

There was something about those classrooms that sent a bad omen my way. I just couldn't get it right over there. My first incident was early on in Boot. During class, I raised my hand to get the attention of one of the roaming sergeants. I asked to use the latrine and was granted permission. While on my way (being escorted no less,) both the sergeant and I passed a commanding officer; I believe he was a lieutenant. I saluted and so did the sergeant, but I dropped my salute before the officer did. Here, again, was quite a comical sight. If you can imaging both of them still standing there holding a hand salute, while I was down and already on my way. I just knew I did something wrong by the look of their faces......like, "The nerve of this grunt." Brows all knitted and shit. My expression was like.........."Why are your hands still up there?" Then thinking, "Damn, where did I go wrong on this one?" The officer bawled out the sergeant, "You incompetent asshole! Teach her right!!" Then yep, the yelling, the screaming and the motivational exercises commenced. Glad, though, he allowed me to first pee. Once again, in that environment, you're real glad for small favors. When I could no longer push myself up or lift my feet (scissor cuts), he sent me off on a solo run (keeping me in visual contact.) "OK soldier, take it down to that building, then over to those trucks, down to the Chapel, then back here. Once back, you better be able to beat your mug 30 times." Those damn punishment counts were never the number initially requested. The sergeants would repeat some of the numbers and sometimes even go backwards in count before regaining a normal count. God damn it! I got back from the run, was knocking out those pushups, and by my count I was on 38. By his count, he was on 24. Of course, I collapsed before 30 (his count) so there I was running again and again and again. After each set was the old favorite "Thank you, Drill Sergeant for strengthening my mind and my body. Feel free to do so at any time."

Next screw up was entering the classroom with my soft cap on. Well I just didn't enter. I walked in a good ways. I was well inside the door when I heard. "Company Halt." All 150 of us came to a halt. I then heard the thumping of boots behind me getting closer. The closer the sound got, the more my heart raced. "Please God, let it not be me they are after. Oh please, please, please." No such luck. There was a violent pull on my collar, then I was pushed and booted outside like a common disorderly drunk from a bar. Now, you have to understand this was in the maybe fifth or sixth week of Boot, so my tolerance for this kind of physical violation was extremely short. Fuel to the fire was my ego. I was platoon leader by that time and I sure didn't appreciate being embarrassed like that in front of my entire platoon, for what I thought at the time was nothing. When he shoved me through the door, I regained my balance, turned around and closed-fisted charged right back at him. Boy, was he quick. Sergeant Thompson did a quick Aikido side-step, grabbed the bib of my cap, whipped it off my head, and slapped me in the face something fierce with it. Ouch. That stopped me dead in my tracks; enough for a reality check: 1) I can never strike an NCO, 2) Since my cap was apparently on my head, I was at fault here, 3) He would kick my ass and lock me up if I continued with this outburst. I snapped to at-ease, and without prompting said "Thank you, Drill Sergeant for strengthening my mind and my body, feel free to do so at any time." He then threw my cap in my face and said, "Come with me, Private." The incident wasn't taken further than the motivational lot. He just kept saying up, down, up, down, up, down......turn over, hold it,—hold it,—hold it. OK, turn over, up, down, up, down, up, down......We kept at this until I threw up.

The third memorable fuck-up was there again in class. I was so exhausted, (that was before I started using speed.) But, I didn't think, though, I was that bad off that I needed to raise my hand and ask permission to stand to the back of the class. So, I reached for my canteen, put it to my mouth, then unfortunately, nodded off while the water was on its way from canteen to lips. My head went back, water went down my trachea, and I lost a grip on the canteen (it fell into my lap.) As my crotch and chair were getting watered, I then started uncontrollably coughing. Believe me, I tried so hard to stop or muffle my coughing as quickly as possible-to a point where I felt my head was going to blow off. Once physically able, I picked up my eyeballs (smile), nervously screwed back on the canteen top, and holstered the canteen; just hoping, please God maybe this breach was not so bad. Maybe they will just let this one go. Maybe they didn't see or hear me.

Nope.

No such luck. The Drill sergeant just pointed and signaled for me to excuse my soggy crotch and myself from the class. More of the same-up, down, up, down, run here, run there. Shit!

Afternoon chow was either in the field or in the mess hall. Evening chow was rarely away from the mess hall. Everywhere we went we were marched there in cadence. The only real breather we got Monday through Saturday was after evening chow. We hung around the barracks just doing a variety of stuff. Some of us lifted weights, some of us practiced drills, some wrote letters, some read, some began shining their boots, and still others did their laundry. Mail-call was around that time also. If a soldier got edible care packages, she had to share it with first her squad, then the platoon. If we were sleeping with our weapons that evening, we would be disassembling and cleaning them, otherwise we would be returning them to the armory. Later in the evening we took our showers but we were not allowed to turn down our bunks to sleep until 2200. At that time, the first fire guard was on post. She had to be dressed in her full BDUs and basically, she walked the barracks for an hour making sure no one went AWOL and that no fires broke out. Fifteen minutes before her shift was over she would wake the next one on duty to start getting up and ready. Some of us had to pull Company guard duty. That required live ammo. At the beginning of Boot we paced the area with a soldier from another company who was authorized to carry a loaded weapon. Later into training we could solo guard with our weapons. When on Company guard, if we saw or heard movement, we were to first un-shoulder our weapon and say "Halt! Who goes there?" The person *should* halt. If they were not yet in view, our next order was, "Step forward to be recognized." They *should* do so. Next was, "Put your identification on the ground in front of you, take six steps back, and halt!" At that point we shouldered our weapon, stepped forward and picked up the identification, confirmed their identity and/or escorted them to the MP station. This is the morbid part. If the detainee disobeys, those are immediate grounds to discharge our weapons. Every U.S. soldier knows the drill and knows the consequences. Therefore, for someone to approach you or run, they definitely are not soldiers and definitely do not belong on the United States Army base. Although your life may not directly be threatened, the security of the base may be compromised. Pretty clear cut and very straight forward.

Since no lone soldiers are supposed to be out that time of night, one really got to use this non-threatening, power-trip drill. BUT of course, I had to be the lucky one to come across Private Jones trying to go AWOL. Apparently, she slipped out without the fireguard seeing her. I heard boots in the grass. I remembered thinking, "Oh, for the love of Jesus. Tell me that someone's not approaching. Well, maybe the Drill sergeant is testing me." So I moved slowly towards the sound until I felt I was close enough to start the drill. "Halt! Who goes there?" Surprisingly, the sound stopped. I am now thinking, 'Yeah buddy, this stuff really works.' "Step forward to be recognized." She did. I recognized her from First Platoon. It then occurred to me that this wasn't a test. Although I recognized her, I continued, "Put your identification on the ground in front of you, take six steps back and halt." She did. As I approached her and her ID, I noticed she didn't look good. She was dusty, her soft cap was not on straight and her collar wasn't evenly turned. It also looked like she had been crying. As I bent down to pick up her ID, she started to approach me. Oh boy, big mistake. Again if a soldier approaches you after that order is given to, "take six steps back and halt," then, that person is not a soldier. It was the craziest, most intense, in-your-face choice for a seventeen year-old have to make. It didn't take too many steps for her to be on me; close enough to possibly disarm me. So in seeing the movement in front of me, and knowing my orders, I should have immediately capped her. I quickly shuffled back (almost tripping myself up,) cocked my weapon, took off the safety; then put sights and barrel right to her chest. So many things flew through my mind in a millisecond. First, I was taken by surprise, so the first thing I knew to do was my duty.........shoot. But I saw the fear in her eyes (like.........shit, man. Did I fuck up!) Most importantly, I knew her, so therefore she belonged on Company area. But, knowing the consequence of approaching without authorization, what the hell was she doing? She just froze. I just froze. Both of us stood there for a while until I again took control of the situation. Shaking like a leaf, I told her immediately, "Lay eagle." She did. I took a look at her military ID card which definitely checked out. I asked her if she was dope-crazy or something; being out there trying to get herself shot? She told me in a calm but very direct tone that she fought off the sergeants, she was tired of the bullshit, and that she was going home. Oh my God, I knew exactly what she was talking about. She did what all of us were so scared of doing...fighting back. She was not going to allow them to take away her last sense of modesty; her own sacredness. I knew she was up Shit Creek if she went back to her platoon, but I would be in a whole heap of trouble if I pretended not to see her. Someone would have broken my post. I apologized profusely and radioed Company Post Headquarters (CPHQ) to send the military police. I remember telling her that maybe someone at C.Q. would listen to her and possibly transfer her to another company. Whatever the case was, I never saw Private Jones again.

7

Sunday: Day of Worship and Prayer

Sundays were the days we looked forward to most. We got to sleep until 0500 and didn't have PT to look forward to. It was a day of lounging. Once again, small favors were a welcome gift. The day started with an organized, cadence driven-march over to the Supply Depot to turn in our used bed linens and to pick up new ones. Then at around 0700 was Chapel. Funny even, for avid churchgoers, 7:00 a.m. mass was crazy-early to be praising the Lord. Nevertheless, things were real turned-on-its-head in the Army. 0700 was like 11:00 am civilian time considering what time we were usually up and how much we would have done by then. Anyway, even if you weren't really religious, it would behoove a soldier to attend Chapel services. Chapel was the only place during Boot that men and women could fraternize. If someone chose not to partake, then they were suspected to be gay. Weird, huh? Chapel became the proving ground of heterosexuality, or a closet for homosexuality. On Sunday mornings you would find us women trying our best to look exceptionally good; minus our makeup, blow dryers, perfume, hair curlers, and jewelry. It was pretty tough, but we all gave it a good try. This meant extra scrubbing in the shower, more care in combing our hair, making sure our eyebrows were brushed, BDU tops pulled to taper at the waist, and teeth extra brushed. Oh the pain; oh the stupidity.

Before services, there was a mini-social where punch and cookies were served. What a meat market! We all knew that we had only, like,

30 minutes to talk and cuddle. We would scope each other out, make visual contact, jump straight from "my name is......" to holding hands, to finding a corner to smooch in. I met a guy, Tony, there my first week at Chapel who was in his forth week. It was never asked if we were committed to someone in the real world or not. We both just needed companionship. Though there was no overt groping, actual foreplay, grinding or sex, there was a lot of body contact in the form of, stroking, squeezing, kissing and hugging. As our platoon came marching up, you could see the guys already there at Chapel tripping over themselves at the Chapel door. It made us women feel attractive again and, I guess, gave the men a sense of "being manly."

When services began, the men and women would separate by the church middle aisle, and every Sunday service would begin with "Onward Christian Soldiers;" the same song to conclude. After services, we would have around 15 minutes to finish socializing before the Drill Sergeants came in one-by-one for their platoons. Out of reverence to the Church, they would refrain from cursing. They would just call out the Company letter and Platoon number.

We always looked forward to the long kisses goodbye.

One Sunday, Tony broke down in my arms. Half-assed kissing my neck, he just sobbed and sobbed. He mumbled like a teenaged kid, "I can't take it no more. This place is going to kill me." My God, I thought. Here is this 6'3" grown man, strong, strapping muscle of a brute crying like an old lady. I just held him harder and firmer. I asked him what happened and once I got him talking about the week, it apparently made things a bit lighter. He said that he couldn't do anything right. The Drill Sergeant was beating on him, his squad was constantly messing up, his platoon leader was blaming him for everything, he had to fall out on one of their runs because he was carrying a buddy of his, he was living amongst heathens, his faith in a God was being tried, faith in himself was being tried, he missed his wife and he missed his babies back home.

Awkward moment....a sobbing brute of a man, a *wife*, babies, my neck being nibbled on, and his hands already down the back of my pants.

Yet...

"It's alright, Tony. There, there, Tony. Just a few more weeks, Sweetie. Buck up now, buck up. You can make it. Come on now, who's my big papa bear?"

...like, whatever.

Is cheating or this type of behavior justified or condonable in the eyes of secular morality? Does society turn a blind eye when one is incarcerated, at war or going through a major transformation similar to Boot camp? Am I a bad person in entertaining Tony's advances and making advances of my own? How far does one go until "it" is termed "disrespecting a relationship;" a union made under God....in the house of God, no less? Is it conceivable that we could go through something as traumatic as Boot without some form of comforting by another human who understands our plight? At the time, I justified my actions, after hearing about the wife and babies, in that I did not want to break up his marriage, and most importantly, as he, I so needed to feel warm, protected, and attractive in a cold, unprotected, and ugly place. Not that I didn't think about it, but, it just would have been career suicide if I sought this type of relationship in the barrack itself.

The rest of the day on Sundays was spent cutting the grass on company grounds, writing letters, preparing assignments for class the upcoming week, or attending sessions offered by visiting psychologists. Civilian psychologists and sometimes uniformed psychiatrists would come in and conduct therapy sessions for those of us who felt like attending. We could freely talk about the mistreatment, our fears, and our past issues...things like that. Although we would beg the civilian psychologists (different ones every week) to do something about the treatment of us women (referring to things like the rape issue.), every time they seemed so appalled and promised results. We would wait for some form of reform, but it never came. Another week would pass, a few more women would be sexually assaulted, and the wall closed in tighter. Sunday would roll around again and we would all be in tears begging for the world to pay attention to our woes. Still nothing. Maybe they are bound to some form of confidentiality. Maybe we were merely research rats for their grand papers of women in the military. I do not know. All I knew was nothing was done. I guess they were just a bunch of puppets for the system; every last one of them. In my opinion, they were good-for nothing mental health workers.

Organized fights were also encouraged on Sundays. Almost certainly on Monday I was plagued with something swollen; my knuckles, my eyes or my lip, a banged up knee, scraped elbow, or a splitting headache.

Oh, almost forgot to tell you. On Sunday morning, we would pile up on brown bombers…laxatives. Most of us, because of the stress and dehydration of the week prior would be severely constipated. So on Sundays with free reign of the latrine and unrestricted visits to the John, we would try and solve the problem with laxatives. Like that wasn't making us even more dehydrated.

So my Sundays were spent being a knowing participant to the erosion of the martial relationship, fighting, defecating like a banshee, and talking with shrinks. And this was the day we looked forward to.

8

The Disco Hut

In about the third week of Boot we were exposed to a concentrated form of tear gas. The official name of the exercise was Nuclear Biological Chemical Training. Up to now I still really do not know the real purpose for this exercise. Maybe it was to document our reaction to intense discomfort. Maybe it was to teach us how to control and prevent panic. Maybe it was to expose us to a form of chemical warfare so we know what to expect. Hell man, maybe it was for shits and giggles. I don't know. From the first week, we heard of the infamous "disco hut," sometimes called the gas chamber. The exercise was given that colorful name by those before us because the fumes in the tear gas shed (hut) would make you uncontrollably dance (gyrate.) What does she mean by that, you're probably asking?

O.K., fair enough. Explanation follows:

Although well protected, the fumes would seep into your protective garments after a few seconds of exposure and make your skin feel like it was on fire. Scratching, we knew, would make the situation worse because our nails would render the skin more susceptible to the fumes. Eventually, you would give in and start twitching involuntarily; desperately trying not to scratch. The twitching soon escalates to jumping up and down, teeth clenching, knees shaking, head rattling back and forth, shoulders vibrating, and arms shivering; the total effect creating very unique and artistic movements, dubbed the gig or the hut dance. The whole experience was, hence, called the Disco Hut.

As usual I seemed to make situations so much worse than they needed to be. Remember the first day of Boot, when I was punished for not checking my gear, and got back to the barracks and started crying?

Ummm…Yep, you got it. No filters in the gas mask.

Before entering the Disco Hut we were instructed to suit up in our Chemical Warfare gear and secure our gas masks. We would then file into the Hut in groups of 10 or 15. When directed one by one, we were to first take a deep breath, close our eyes, remove our masks, then calmly state our name, rank, serial number, and hometown. After that, we would calmly exit the Hut before our, now open eyes, completely tear up; blinding us and/or before we pass out. Tear gas doesn't just make your eyes tear up, like crying at a sad movie. This is what really happens. It intensely burns your eyeballs and in response, you see, the body produces what we have termed *tears* in order to wash this burning chemical from them. The tear secretion is like nothing you have ever experienced. It's like someone turned on a faucet in your eyes. It just pours out flowing uncontrollably over your lids and down your face. Truly, I was like a waterfall. If breathed in, it first feels like your trachea and bronchial tubes suddenly constrict, blocking any possible chance of inhalation. Second, from the initially-inhaled fumes, your chest feels like a thousand mosquitoes invaded your lungs. What I mean by that is that your chest itches internally, like behind your ribs and sternum. A place you can never physically reach; yet you would still try. At this point, clawing at your chest, you can't cough because the exhalation mechanism is not working in your favor. You just slouch over, looking like you are having dry heaves. You may pass out at this point, or, more typically one of the sergeants would grab you and coldly shove your blind, heaving body outside, where you would eventually recover.

O.K., so there I was in line getting closer to the Hut's door knowing damn well my mask had no filters and seeing the heaving pathetics being thrown out of the far end of the Hut (and they HAD filters.) Option One: say nothing, walk in the hut and try to hold my breath until asked to do and say what I needed to. Impossible! Even if I could hold my breath until it was my turn, I would eventually, in the Hut no less, want to take a breath prior or after the name, number, and city task. It would probably be a big breath since I would be out of air. That means a lung FULL of unfiltered tear gas. Indeed, I would pass out before they could throw me out. Option Two: say something and get hammered in front of the entire company for waiting four friggin' weeks to completely check my gear. As I was pondering my options, my place in line got ever closer and closer.

Finally, I just stepped out of line; still not knowing which one of the bastard drill sergeants I would give the pleasure of humiliating me. Scared, embarrassed and ashamed I didn't direct my attention to any of them. A moment of shear insanity overcame my brain. I just fell out of line and started walking away. Where, in particular did not matter, as long as it was away from the Hut and them. Comically, I heard those bastards behind me. "What the fuck is she…" "Hey you, STOP, HALT!" "STAND AT EASE." "Get back here." "Where the hell does she think she is going?" I just kept walking and as a matter of fact, picked up the pace when I heard the boots thumping behind me. Finally, I was thrown to the ground. Lying there in a pitiful state, I struggled to my knees, and proceeded to crawl in the same direction as I was walking before; with no acknowledgement of what just happened. Again, I was thrown down. "On your feet." With one drill sergeant behind me and another now in front of me, I got to at-ease. Whimpering, I said, "I *r-r-really* can not go into that Hut." He called me a pussy and ordered me to the front of the line. I staggered back to the Hut, turned around and again, walked like a woman truly insane, away from them and the Hut. Boom!! Tackled again. Oh, by that time I had made quite the spectacle of myself. Before I got to my feet, I tore off my mask, as if completely inconvenienced by their attempts to stop my escape, and stammered, "M-m-m-my mask don't have no f-f-fucking filters m-m-man." Those in voice range of me just tore down laughing including the linebacker sergeant. He yelled to the rest of his cronies, "The pussy has no filters!" Now everyone seemed to be laughing at me. You know that was the only break given to me during Boot; so to speak. Someone came over with filters. The bastard sergeant himself showed me how to insert them. He dusted me off and then escorted me to front of the line. The rest of the Disco Hut experience went by event-less. Granted, I did the Disco gig once inside, but when it came my turn, I took a deep *filtered* breath, said my name, rank, serial number, and hometown, and exited without incident. A number of my comrades didn't fair as well in the Hut itself, but they didn't make an ass of themselves beforehand, now did they?

9

The Range

In the 3rd week of Basic Training we were issued our beautiful M-16 A-1 rifles. These were our weapons; extensions of our fists. In a time of conflict, if we discharged our weapons, it would be to kill another human being. There were no warning shot, aiming for the legs or any code of conduct of not shooting a person in the back. None of that. Shoot and shoot to kill.

We have a term for this,…homicide, Right? However you look at it, criminal (manslaughter and murder) or non-criminal (excusable and justifiable homicide), it is the taking of a person's life. Manslaughter is the unlawful killing of another, with no prior malice. Murder is the killing of another, but it requires intent and premeditation, or just intent with no premeditation. Excusable homicide results from an act that normally would not cause death, but because of the victim's negligence, resulted in death. Justifiable homicide includes capital punishment and death caused by a police officer while attempting to prevent a dangerous felon's escape or to capture a dangerous felon who has escaped or is resisting arrest. Killing an enemy during wartime is also classified as justifiable homicide. So, suffice to say that the difference between murder and justifiable homicide could come down to man-made laws; killing and more so murder, being so engrained as a mortal sin. For example, execution of a prisoner in a state banning capital punishment is murder. Just across the border or the following year, it could be justifiable homicide. If you see or sense the enemy, decide or receive orders to eliminate this enemy by opening live rounds, follow through with that decision or order, and accomplish the task, by definition, that constitutes the intentional and premeditated act of taking another human's life...*murder*; that is if war has not officially been declared. Is that the case, though? No! The line between the two is definitely blurred.

As rationally thinking individuals (when first given our rifles), the issue of firing it and possibly killing with it is what we wrestled with. But, as soldiers (after the transformation), killing or "homicide" is glorified, applauded, anticipated, and yes, justified, in most cases.

As soldiers we were forbidden to call our rifles, "guns". I guess the Army or military as a whole wants to make the distinction between firearms used in sport shooting, skeet shooting or game hunting, and those used in war or civil unrest. The M16-A1 rifle caliber of 5.56mm is 39 inches long and 7.6 lbs. loaded. The magazine holds 20 rounds with a maximum range of 2,653 meters and the maximum effective range is 460 meters. The weapon fires 650–700 rounds per minute. Today the M-16-A2 rifle is in use; an improved version of the A-1; a rifle very similar except that it is a little longer, sleeker in appearance, and unfortunately 2 lbs. heavier.

Basic Rifle Marksmanship (BRM) Fundamentals Training lasted about two weeks. Prior to getting to the firing range we were first instructed on how the weapon itself worked. We were taught all it parts: the buttstock, the bolt carrier, the charging handle, the hammer, the trigger, the hand guard, the barrel, the sights, the upper receiver, etc. We learned how to field-strip the rifle so well we could do it in the dark. It was extremely important to keep the weapon clean. Quite frankly, if mud or debris even partially clogged the barrel, upon pulling the trigger, the weapon may explode. BRM involved classroom training and training in the field. A soldier needed to first zero his/her weapon and at the end of the two weeks qualify with their weapon. Sounds like gibberish I know, so I'll break it down for you. Zeroing the weapon means to align the fire control system or your sight with the rifle barrel. When this is accomplished correctly, the point of aim is the point of bullet impact at the standard sight zero range of 300 meters.

During BRM training the soldier exercises with single and multiple targets that are 75 meters, 175 meters and 300 meters down range. The target is a head and shoulder silhouette. To "qualify" the soldier is exposed to 40 targets between 50–100 meters away. Twenty-three hits would qualify you as a marksman. Thirty hits would qualify you as a sharpshooter and thirty-six hits gave you the "expert" designation.

The firing range was a good four miles from the barracks. The march time was a challenging hour and many couldn't make it. You see, after chow and picking up the weapons from the armory, we would get into full gear including steel pot and rucksack. Our equipment and weapons were challenging to carry for four miles at a quick step. Some days were outrageously hot and with the added weight, people were passing out left and right, and falling out of formation to throw up. Thank goodness it wasn't like PT where the formation had to keep turning around until the soldier got back in. For the slacker, it actually was worse. A covered truck would come and pick up the slacker and transport her in comfort to the field range. Why was that worse you might be asking yourself? Well, imagine you being on that hot road, gutting it out, sweating, puking, and dragging your sun-beaten staggering ass to the range. After four miles or so, you and your buddies see Pvt. Good-for-Nothing sitting in the shade waiting for the Company to arrive; all nice and rested without a trace of sweat. I believe there would be a certain amount of animosity. It is that animosity that the Drill Sergeants milked. They could have punished the soldier by leaving her along the roadside or having her do a whole punch of push-ups and stuff but, no. They purposely took very good care of her so as to piss off the rest of us. They put the soldier on display in the shade. Given the chance, (usually during R&R) we would all try to kick this soldier's ass. You lose friends and you have over 100 women after you. I saw some women screaming as so not to be put in the covered trunk; trying to continue the foot march even though they already started to poop on themselves (oh, that's what happens when you're past the point of exhaustion; loss of bowl control).

Once live rounds were handed out, a whole bunch of precautions were taken. Every action was done on command and our every move guarded. "Remove the empty magazine. Place the weapon on the sandbag with barrel down range. Take 2 steps back. Stop. Take first bullet from pouch and load in magazine. Take second bullet out. Load in magazine, pick up weapon and face down range. Lock and load. Take position in foxhole. Take aim. You may now discharge your weapon." We shot prone, standing, and from a foxhole. As I recall, though, I sucked at BRM. Matter of fact, I qualified at 23. Go figure.

After each series of shots, we were ordered to place our weapons down and do an about-face. At that time the sergeants would crawl out of their rat holes and scamper down to the silhouettes. If, let's say, you kept a couple of rounds in your weapon and felt compelled to use them on one of the sergeants. Ah, well, the tower guard would shoot you dead. If someone turned around any at all, the tower guard would sound the alarm and take aim. The sergeants, hearing the alarm, would hit the deck. Not cool when they were in full stride to have to hit the deck.

Not only were we trained on the rifle, but also on the 9mm side arm, M-60 machine gun and the grenade launcher. Despite my ineptness, I loved firing my rifle. I loved the smell of the powder, the feel of the buttstock as the weapon kicked, the moment of stillness (like your heart stops) just before I pulled the trigger. But, there was one element about the range though that did not exactly stand out as a pleasant experience. I believe you may agree with me, unless of course you are a closeted coprophiliac.

The latrines at the range were as crude as civilized crude could be. For all the female soldiers on the range there was only one long hut to be used as a latrine. Upon entering this hut, the smell of an unkempt outhouse steaming with stale piss saturated shit hits you like black exhaust smoke. Although invisible, you wonder how you didn't see the smoke coming. Your eyes squint; the insides of your nostrils constrict; you are stopped dead in your tracks. Then, you taste the odor in your mouth; on your tongue; oozing from your pores. Sweat beads accumulate on your forehead and finally your stomach turns inside out. Some women chose not to go in after being hit with the horrendous smell outside the hut. "I will pass out if I take another step. "Oh h-h-h-hell no." "I-I think I am going to fucking barf." Unfortunately, most of those women eventually peed on themselves or embarrassed themselves by resorting to a frantic don't give-a-damn dropping of their trousers and squat pissing somewhere on the range or on their way back to the barracks; ass in the breeze, yes. One of the many freedoms a soldier gives up in Boot is the freedom to go to the restroom whenever is convenient. I know most of you take it for granted. I did. In civilian life, let's say in a meeting, you would excuse yourself, maybe even awkwardly, to go when you really gotta go. At school, you may have to somewhat embarrass yourself by asking "permission" to leave the classroom and visit the washroom. But, a meeting facilitator or instructor will not deny you that right. Alone and on your own agenda, it is just the matter of finding a bathroom that fits your standards; a highway rest area, a gas station bathroom, a Dunkin' Donuts or fast-food restaurant bathroom, a mall rest room, etc. While "in" when you got the opportunity to use the latrine or a location that somewhat preserved your modesty from the opposite sex and your boots from your own urine, eventually you learned to take advantage of the privilege. You really did not know when again you may be allowed to go. If it didn't fit into Drill Sergeant X's schedule, then a soldier was stuck doing a bathroom gig, holding their crotch, soiling their trousers, running to a bush, or just squatting right where they were.

Anyway, back to the range latrine. In the hut there were two wide slabs of wood with about sixteen holes each (eight pairs) lengthwise in the one steamy room. These holes were elevated to around knee height on what looked like two, long, wide, plywood boxes. There were no toilet seats nor lids; no partitions, no handles, no rails, no semblance of privacy, not even a chalk-drawn line of separation between one hole and another. My God, if you dared to sit on the filthy slab of molding, diseased, festering wood and leaned back, for certain you would make contact with the person voiding or defecating behind you. A set of 32 soldiers was marched in first, and as one left, another soldier was permitted in. Therefore the latrine was always nice and packed. It seemed everywhere we went we needed a chaperone; a Drill (female) Sergeant at the latrine door permitting soldiers in one by one (with the exception of the initial 32.) Back to back and side to side we all just kind of squatted over our holes hoping that our asses would not touch. The others in line just watched at the door, scratching their noses and getting all teary eyed from the smell. Those who were menstruating would have to bear it all. They would either pull out the saturated tampon, drop it in the hole and insert another, or tear their soiled pad off, throw it down the hole, then with panties by their knees, affix another. It was plumb nasty to see and worse to be put in that position. Like, what can you do?

Needless to say, there was no toilet paper. Therefore, we had to either drip dry or plan ahead by carry some paper from the barracks. Oh, no sink either…So think about that. Yummy.

I am sure they must clean the range latrine at some point by maybe hosing down the interior and draining the boxes. Nevertheless, I really didn't understand how almost everything else surrounding our existence at Boot was so sterile; the barracks, the barrack latrine, the mess hall, the linens, and in contrast the range was so nasty.

At the end of the day we all were thoroughly searched for any ammo, had to clean our weapons, then return them to the armory unless pulling guard that night. Considering how beat up and angry we all were, I am actually surprised no one fired on the sergeants during my rotation through Basic. Many a time I thought of it. My plan was to refrain from discharging my weapon three times so I would have those rounds to work with when those bastards came out of hiding. I would shoot the tower guard first, and then turn and shoot the two NCOs that made my life a living hell as they slowed down to visibly investigate the blast behind them. One major problem with my plan though. I couldn't shoot worth shit.

10

Fights

U pon arriving at Basic Training, most of us were filled with all sorts of emotions; excitement, anticipation, enthusiasm, patriotism, and huge egos. Within a few days, those emotions transformed into distrust, suspicion, timidness, fear, anxiety, revengeful sadism, and anger. As recruits being trained to be soldiers, we were quickly, and I dare say, harshly, stripped of our independence, and before we knew what was happening, our freedom as individuals was gone. We could do little without permission and it seemed like everyone was telling us what to do.

Trainees or recruits are at the way bottom of the chain of command; the absolute bottom; the ultimate starting point after one takes the Oath. I mean seriously, in reference to loss of our independence, with the exception of Sundays, we couldn't even go the bathroom unless we asked AND our requests granted. Back to that point I made earlier; things civilians take for granted. We were told what to wear, where to go, what time to sleep, what time to wake, how far to run, when to eat, how to sit, how to move (march), and even "assigned" a buddy.

The Sergeants were completely in charge of our lives and totally lapping-up the power of it all; like fucking thirsty wildebeests after their migration through the African southern desert. Secretly, we all envied this power. The Privates who arrived a few days before I wanted to throw their weight around by telling me, the new comer, what to do; starving for a sense of importance. The soldiers taller, more muscular, and older than I were also picking on me. The white soldiers were trying to boss around the minority soldiers. The athletic ones were messing with the slightly overweight ones. The trickling down effect was obviously in high gear.

Sergeants were constantly verbally abused, taken advantage of, and somewhat humiliated by the commanding officers. So in order to regain some sort of self worth, I suppose, the sergeants would do the same to the buck Private who basically had to take it. The difference, though, was that at least the officers had some semblance of respect for the sergeants; they just enjoyed ragging on them. The sergeants on the other hand didn't have one smidge of respect for us. At times it seemed like they had a vendetta against us because it was obvious that the treatment was no longer training but rather sadistic "fun." In their eyes, we were not yet even soldiers. We had zero time in. I truly believe that some of them were just weak, cowardly people who hid behind their stripes. So in order to establish some sort of worth, they took the lazy way out and took advantage of people who, by military law, could not fight back; lest be severely punished. It was like in John Steinbeck's *Of Mice and Men* when Curley, a scrunt of a man, kept picking on Lenny who was portrayed as mentally challenged. Lenny, in Curley's eyes, seemed weak, vulnerable, and unable to defend himself. He was the only person in the work camp Curley could prove himself with; to be the big man. Moreover, if Lenny fought back he may be fired, given that Curley was the son of the property owner.

Feeling cheated out of the power game, most of us buck privates had no one technically under us that had to take it from us, yet we all still needed a scapegoat, of sorts, for our release (or so we thought.) Hence the inner fighting; exaggerated release of misplaced anger.

Another strong reason for physical aggression at Boot was the overall climate of the Army. We were being trained to fight. Soldiers fight right? But in a time of peace there is no proving ground for the soldier. Everything is train, train, and train some more; take the shit and suck it up. Women got so wrapped up in the proving-ground syndrome, as I like to call it, so any reason was a good reason to throw-down with another.

Back in Junior and Senior High School, I took karate classes and soon became an avid student of the Martial Arts. I practiced Okinawan Uechi Ryu karate, winning a few sparing, kata and weapon trophies. I earned my brown belt just before moving to Florida. There was a strict code of conduct my Sensei expected from all of his students in reference to fighting and boastful display of the Art. However, that code went out the window in the Army when thrown into the peer pressure mess of the proving ground. I actually behaved myself for the first two weeks. I knew I could kick ass but my Sensei taught me compassion, restraint and tolerance; virtues of a true martial artist.

Now, one of the few situations that really got my goat more than anything else was getting hammered for stuff I didn't do. First the motivational exercises were hard as hell, could be painful and most definitely SUCKED. Second, it made me lose face with my squad and platoon, and thirdly it made all my efforts in getting it right, null and void. It was like three slaps in the face. I am ashamed to say that my first fight was over the same issue of shit that I didn't do.

Private Morris was about 5'4" and maybe 115-lbs. soaking wet. She was in my squad and kept doing stuff wrong. Stuff that could be avoided, like she would not sound off in formation; just marching in silence while the others were cadencing. She would constantly get out of step. She would not shine her boots. She would be late getting into formation. She would try and sneak food back to the barracks. Her bunk was never tight enough. Being her squad leader at the time, I would have to shoulder her punishments. She would only be called on her mistakes then, "What squad do you belong to Private?" "3rd Squad, Drill Sergeant," Ok, 3rd squad leader, front and center, beat your mug, Private Forbes." First, I tried talking with her but that didn't work. I tried verbally scolding her. That too didn't work.

One evening she racked up so many demerits, that I was out in the dirt for over an hour. When I came back into the barracks she was laughing it up with her buddies. Some of my friends huddled around me to see if I was OK. One said, "Forbsy, like, what the fuck?" That's all it took. Calmly, I walked over to Pvt. Morris, with one hand grabbed her by her BDU collar and dragged her into the barracks latrine. Her friends jumped to their feet but did nothing. They just stood there watching me pull away Morris. The latrine had two or three steps that led down into it. When I threw her in, she tripped giving me time to turn and say to the curious mass, "No one is to come in here for a while." You have to remember that up to then no one knew I practiced karate, no one knew I had a temper. The platoon just looked at me like I had gone insane. I closed the door slowly behind me and approached Morris. I exchanged no words with her as she got to her feet, with attitude. From the door my eyes sealed on hers and with quick decisive steps, I walked through her with a forward push. When our bodies touched, Morris went flying and hit the sinks behind her. That stunned her but didn't ground her. The attitude she cocked before was now gone. She came towards me (or made a run for the door behind me) and I met her square. I quickly found out that she was the type of fighter that blindly runs and tackles. Few women stand and slug it out. Most, though, wildly swing with hopes of scratching or slapping hard enough to inflict pain or something. She apparently preferred wrestling. Since that was the case, I needed to definitely stay on my feet and keep her in an unfamiliar place. She grabbed me around the waist and pushed me back against the wall. Still keeping a clear head, I hammer-fisted her precisely at the base of the skull. She fell immediately to her knees. It was easy after that. I just threw her around like a rag doll. Picked her up by the collar and threw her against the sinks. When she tried to crawl away, I humiliatingly slapped the top of her head or kicked her rear end, then grabbed her and threw her the other way. The whole time I kept thinking, "This is way too easy." It felt so good I cannot begin to tell you. As she hit the laundry machines, it would make a loud thud. I could hear the oohs outside the door. Finally, she started crying and saying "Forbsy, I'm sorry. I'm sorry. I'll do better." No words on my part. I stopped, checked if I lost any buttons and walked out of the latrine. My only regret with that fight was not having an audience. Oh, it was worth seeing.

You may be asking "What about Pvt. Morris, huh?" Well, she had a few bruises, a sprained wrist and a few detached buttons, as I remember. She straightened up and could do no wrong after that. Mission accomplished. My squad either started to fear me or respect me. Either way they knew they were going to be in a world of pain if they fucked up. But they also knew I had their back. This came from an incident that happened actually a few days after Morris' beating.

I heard words being exchanged between one woman from my squad, Pvt. Spitzmeister and a soldier from another platoon. It seemed so one sided. Whatever was previously done, Spitz was saying, "hey, I'm sorry" and the other was still laying into her harping on whatever. I stepped in to mediate. After all, she was part of my squad and platoon, and I happened to be her squad leader. The woman turned on me. Unlike Morris, this one was a big woman. She just got all up in my face as I was telling her to back off of Spitz. Then came the oh-so-common, "what you gonna do bitch…huh? Well, what you gonna do?" So once again, no words were uttered on my part after that. I forcefully pushed her away from me but as I pushed her, I followed her back-peddling, then clocked her dead on the nose; well more along the lines of the side of the nose and cheek bone. Most people make the mistake by pushing their opponent back and then they too taking a step back (in the opposite direction) to gloat or to see what their adversary will do. Usually, not too many people back down from a push, so, as for what will they do? They will regroup and come back at ya. Right? As for the gloating, well, whatever. Someone, who has lost their footing or is off balance, cannot protect him or herself as effectively. This is the best opportunity to fire off your best placed and hardest hit.

Her arms immediately moved up to her nose as she hunched over. I couldn't really go for her mid section because her forearm shielded that area. Given my choices, I closed fisted her to the temple/ear area a few times before she finally fell. She tried to protect herself but I wasn't through with her. At that point I fired off a cruel flaying kick to her covered face which sent her flying straight back. Now I had an audience and I was not going to let it go to waste. I needed a message to be sent. So as she lay there, I knelt beside her and said soft enough that it didn't seem like a performance, but loud enough that those close could hear, "Don't fuck with my squad. Are we clear on that?"

A few more fights followed but they were more along the lines of personal challenges.

Hell, I guess word got around and it was time for a lesson in humility. One day during evening chow, the drill sergeant called me over to the sergeant's mess table. I rushed over and snapped to at-ease. Smirking, he said that he saw in my file that I practiced karate and even put it down as my hobby. I said, "Yes, drill sergeant." There are usually only three responses to directives and questions from the drill sergeant. They are, "yes drill sergeant," "no drill sergeant," and "I have no excuse drill sergeant." Given the question asked, I answered truthfully and bit arrogantly, "Yes drill sergeant." He started in on me saying, "So you think you are the shit then, Private?" I smirked back at him and again said, "Yes drill sergeant." "Very well, finish up and meet us outside, Private." Oops, what had I done?

What the sergeant did was to organize a fight between a female drill sergeant and myself. I have a feeling it was actually already in the works and he just egged me on; had me dig my own arrogant pretentious grave. You would think that this kind of stuff doesn't go on in the military, but it does. Not just between enlistees or buck privates, but actually organized, supported, and encouraged by those who are charged with the responsibility of keeping order and upholding policies. You would think that there is an oversight committee of sorts that polices stuff like this. I am sure there is, but it is certainly not visible on the base.

So there I was, after chow, facing someone who did me no harm, or I her. The only reason we were fighting was because of the familiar proving ground. Who is tougher? Stupid statements to be made. Symbolically, she took off her drill sergeant's hat. I took off my boots. From previous fights, I found that I could sweep quicker, move faster, and was more agile without those heavy boots. I once mentioned something about an audience. Well here it was; Privates, Sergeants and Commanding officers alike waiting for a show. Yep, dear old Forbsy in the middle of it all. What ever happened to the shy little girl in the pastel nighty?

The sergeant and I circled each other for a while but I couldn't get a feel of what type of fighter she was. She moved with a sense of familiarity and confidence. I remember thinking, "Fuck it, let's get this over with." I stepped in, faked a left dab and clocked her quickly but apparently not too solidly across her left jaw. She blinked. Then from nowhere my face exploded and I went down. Didn't even see it coming. Up to now I don't know where she got that bat (smile.) Nah, there was no bat, just fast hands. Dazed and embarrassed as all get out, I struggled to my knees. Then my side exploded from a kick and all I remember was trying to breathe. Holding my ribs and gasping, I heard, in the distance, my platoon being led away by an unfamiliar female cadence caller. When I opened my eyes, I was alone. The dirt had settled and mess hall door was closed. It was like a dream. There was no evidence of what just occurred. It was like hitting a deer on the highway; a deer that staggered away post accident. You are stranded in the middle of nowhere; car can't operate, car obviously damaged but nothing to evidence the accident.

What to do? I painfully got to my feet, somewhat dusted myself off, and walked back to the barracks, feeling like a fish out of water. When I got to the barracks, my buddies just looked at me and continued going about their business. They were ashamed of me, and, I guess I of myself. Forbes yes, got her ass kicked in close to eight seconds flat. Needless to say, no more fights followed that incident. Whatever I had to prove, thank goodness, was already proven, and I was reluctant to initiate anything again.

Lesson learned.

Was my beat-down justified? I think so. Was Morris' beat down justified? Oh most definitely, I think. What do you think?

11

Suicide

We all have our breaking point. Some, though, reach it before others. Granted, many a nights I cried rivers. I thought of heading in one direction with hopes of finding the base exit. Many a day I thought of shooting the Drill Sergeants. I thought of shooting myself on several occasions. I was just completely over it, over them, over me, over life. The bullshit was endless and getting worse. Hopes of making it out with any kind of previously known self-respect was lost. I was lost. I was becoming an emotionless robot yet still was not completely indoctrinated, so I knew it (the loss of self) was slowly occurring; a train on an unstoppable derailment path. You, as soldiers, were basically ordered to be proud of what *they* created, so you play a part. You fake the "hoo-rah, proud to be a GI shit." Ironically, what they created was who you now were. So you were stuck in your own performance called *shame*.

The conversion happens subtly. The military as a whole has a set of moral codes, values, principles, and ethical and condonable behavior. They drive these principles so hard into the soldier that eventually s/he believes it's their own set of values. Follow me on this please. They took your personal belongings away and all visual reminders of your previous life, they dressed you in the uniform of conformity, they made you deathly frightened of them, they beat you up, they made sure that the punishment was much worse than the task given in order for you to choose the better (the task)of the two evils. Imagine if the task was to lap your morning chow on all fours like a dog by the front door of the mess hall. O.K., that is not only totally disrespectful, but terribly humiliating, and most would say, "No." If the powers-that-be scream at you, you may still say, "no." If they smack you around, you still may refuse. The threat of incarceration may not even work in that case. What may work, you might be asking yourself? I can answer that. They hurt you so bad and they inflict so much pain on you, which was really never-ending, where you "can't take it anymore." Even if you passed out, once you came to, it started all over. It was like a tag team, where when one drill sergeant got tired of giving you the treatment, s/he handed off the responsibility to someone else entering all nice and fresh for round two of the next evolution. It was like entering the boxing ring with a fresh boxer every round. You just eventually broke down and did what they ask so they would stop hurting you. The overpowering of their presence, intensity of the exercises, dowses of water, the forced marches and runs, the hours of standing at attention in our urine saturated trousers, the sexual molestation, the punches, slaps, kicks, and the hopelessness made you do almost anything they ask.

The more severe built on the less severe. In other words, if you claimed to not be able shine your boots properly, they would punish you with pushups. If you claimed to not be able to handle the pushups, they may have stepped on your fingers until you pushed yourself up again. If the finger thing just got you screaming, they would really give you something to scream at like one kick to every uttered sound. I will stop there at go in reverse. You stopped screaming to stop the kicking. You somehow mustered the strength to push yourself up, and your fingers were released from under the boot. The pain of the crushing fingers outweighed the presumed lack of strength. You would shine your boots from hence forth to standard to prevent that from occurring again. As a reminder sometimes, you were punished in a similarly harsh fashion for nothing done wrong; merely to insure that when asked to do something you would reflect on what may truly happen. I guess in the drill sergeant's mind they didn't have time for "cause and effect." They just made sure that we knew the effect, so we would never challenged the cause.

Run and you would be caught. Scream and it will only fall on deaf ears. Funny, we have grown up believing that if we screamed, "Help", help will eventually come. It is a tough reality when you scream help as loudly as you can and no one responds. Guaranteed, when asked again to do another task, you remember what they did to you before and how hopeless a situation that was. Defying a directive does not have similar results as being a civilian. Defying a task at work, for example, may get you fired, but that is a choice you make. You may lose that job, but you have saved your dignity. You stood on principle. When "in" defying only means pain and they will drive you to a point where you will end up doing what you were defying anyway. Dignity and personal principle suddenly have no worth; hence the breakdown in your self-respect, if that is what you build it on. Eventually, an emotionless robot is born. At almost your weakest moment they bombard you with the fact that your life is nothing. Then you believe that it is indeed nothing, because you have no dignity left, no worth, your family is not around, you have no autonomy, you are tired, and you are so tremendously scared. Here is where they totally win. The Army then gives you worth, but it is according to the Army's value system. That becomes all you can hold on to and receive external validation for.

Pvt. Davis was a complainer from day one. "I'm tired of the bull shit," "Can't take this fucking Army," "I don't belong here," "You all hate me," "I hate every last one of you." When she was "motivated" by the Drill Sergeants, she took it harder than the rest of us, and the more she showed her weaknesses, the more the sergeants rode her. One weird night as we were preparing for lights out, Pvt. Davis didn't seem herself. She started giving away personal stuff under the pretense of, "…just doing a little house cleaning." That night she swallowed a whole bunch of pills that she apparently got smuggled in. The morning after, as the platoon was scrambling to get out into formation for PT, Pvt. Davis didn't budge. The Sergeant was alerted, the ambulance was called and Davis was rushed to the base infirmary. Our Platoon Sergeant called us together that evening to what I thought was going to be the announcement that Davis was dead or something to that effect. Maybe a grief counselor would come in to talk with us.

Quite the contrary.

He informed us that we were to be disciplined for Davis' behavior. He said, "Unfortunately, the bitch is still alive. So because you all allowed this to happen, the platoon, for the next three nights from 2200 hours to 0300 (one hour before PT), will remain at at-ease to think about it. If you want to kill yourself, make sure you kill yourself."

In addition, two soldiers had to pull suicide watch at the infirmary at one-hour intervals.

After the first night instead of feeling sorry and empathic towards Davis, we all wanted to wring her neck. She didn't return to the barracks, but if she did, she would have been returning to a pissed off group, I guarantee that. See the reason or rationale for our punishment/discipline yet? If any of us considered a suicide attempt for the sole purpose of getting a little attention (a pity party), it certainly would not end up being that; there would be animosity instead of pity; bitterness instead of compassion; resentfulness instead of sympathy. Needless to say, no one in the barracks, even in jest, spoke of killing themselves again after that.

Still, suicide at some point seemed like the only way out.

12

Rape

This topic, rape, is a difficult one for me, and no, rape is not justified in any context or form.

In the U.S. Army and other branches of the U.S. military, sexual assault and sexual crimes are prevalent. Make no mistake, and I enunciate this plainly and clearly, rape occurs on almost every military base in the nation and on bases abroad. The crimes pass into antiquity without report, punishment, or reprimand. Obviously, there are no accurate crime statistics, and the Army, especially, will deny any allegation of them. But talk with those who have served; those who are strong enough to break the code of silence. For several reasons you, the general civilian population, hear little to nothing about the atrocious behavior of those leading our forces. Many women do not come forward due to fear of reprisal, retaliation, and humiliation.

They have probably already lived through the repercussions of what happens when you squeal. Violent crimes of a sexual nature are so institutionalized that nothing internal is ever done when a complaint gets through to those that could possibly put a stop to it. Army legal service asks for evidence and cooperation, but it is never enough. The case is usually dropped or dismissed. Always comes down to his word over yours. Meanwhile, you and your name will be smeared. Poor evaluations, harassment and violence will, with certainty, follow. If you back a buddy in her fight, you, too, will be harassed. The civilian legal community, by law, cannot interfere if even made aware. Sergeants are posted at every phone during calling privileges so you can't really verbalize a complaint (in the hopes of media attention); well you could,

96

but Lord have Mercy, watch out afterward. You can't mail a letter by yourself. Letters are given to the platoon sergeant and he or she will mail them. Needless to say, letters of various soldiers will not get into the U.S. postal system and/or it may be read.

The psychologists, counselors and doctors at first seem very compassionate when you, on base, break the silence and try and talk to someone about what happened. But, you see, it is not kept in confidence, and next thing you know (a day or two later) you are being slapped around by the whole lot of company sergeants (about eight of them.) You can't do shit right. You are put on all sorts of punishment tasks. You are pulling double guard duty of, let's say, a garbage receptacle or something as senseless as that. You are not given latrine privileges or asked to eat your chow on all fours. You are purposely tripped up doing PT and marches and worst of all, you are taken out again in the middle of the night. Either someone, who is experiencing retaliatory correction, talks to their buddies on the whys behind it or you yourself are going through the shit. Either way, we all learned directly or indirectly what squealing would bring.

Women learned to keep silent. It is weird to even think about it along these lines, but it was worse for us if we squealed. In all honesty, we were better off keeping our mouth shut. We were/are still truly alone legally behind those guarded gates. I mean, think about it. Whistleblowers in civilian life may lose their job, lose their pension and possibly lose any hope of working in the same field again. But at least the whistleblower exposed, let's say, the corporate corruption. Exposure apparently meant more to the individual than the possible loss of their career. In the Army, being a whistleblower didn't mean getting out; it meant staying in the hell, a hell that will only get much more intense and fierce. Then, after all that, still nothing is accomplished. Transfer requests denied.

A friend of mine used her only chance to make a minor complaint to a commanding officer who, she thought, would take some form of moral or just action. She had not learned, as yet, that all of them protect each other; whether they are commissioned or noncommissioned officers. It was during an in-class lecture on the rights and duties of enlisted personnel that a lieutenant was present. She very courteously asked to speak freely. Given permission, she proceeded to file a formal complain concerning vulgar language used towards her and those in the platoon. He said something to the effect of, "I understand. I will look into that." Later that week she was led out in the middle of the night. I know this because she and the platoon sergeant walked right by my bunk. When she returned she was in real bad shape. She forcefully pushed away anyone including myself, who tried to help or comfort her.

Now some of us had already been led away in that fashion, so we knew what probably occurred out there in the dark in some empty barrack against the some rusty locker or bunk rail. Some women screamed and wailed, and quickly got a fist in the mouth for it.

Silence.

I will now bring up a word mentioned before...*obedience.* Do you agree that those who are frightened, weak, timid, and feel like they are in a hopeless situation will submit and comply? Would you? For the most part, the women who were sexually assaulted were attractive, innocent flirts, those who challenged the officers' (non commissioned and commissioned) authority, those who may patronize the Sergeants, or just plain royal screw ups. So let me ask you the reader then, what would be your plan of protection? To me, it seemed obvious; look and behave as unattractive as possible, never dare challenge the authority of your sergeant, react and respond immediately, don't ever look the sergeants in the eye lest they think you are flirting, and try never, ever, to screw up. Hmm, does that kind of sound like what a soldier should be about? Enough said.

13

Intent

After completing eight weeks of Basic Training, if our drill instructors were successful in their job, we were molded into perfect soldiers. Service promotions today say that the military does not want robot soldiers, but rather highly trained thinkers to fight the modern day war, squash terrorism and free those blanketed by repressive governments. What a crock of shit. Yeah, they want thinkers alright; killers who all think the way the military wants them to think. Sounds to me like an educated robot with a weapon. Please don't be fooled by these promotions.

Nadine was lost somewhere around week 6 or 7 and Pvt. Forbes graduated.

I guess I can honestly say that over time I have regained back a sense of individuality as Nadine (Deany), but it is still amazing after eighteen years how quickly Pvt. Forbes just shows up unexpectedly. Metaphorically speaking, I see her face, I recognize her face; a face that is not very pleasant. I ask, "Why are you here." She replies, "Look around you, idiot. Don't you smell that, don't you see that, don't you remember that? Ah, yeah there it is. You remember now, don't ya. I knew you wouldn't ever forget that time we spent in the SHIT together. O.K., bye now. See if you can function normally."

I could hear reveille, let's say, on TV. BAM!! Pvt. Forbes shows up. I could see uniformed personnel on TV, or out and about, or hear a chair being dragged across a tiled floor. She shows up again. I could smell some sort of Alabama or Texan blossom, Pine Sol of all things, or see a small carton of milk. There she is.

After Boot camp there was AIT. Traditionally, A.I.T. were the abbreviations for Advanced Infantry Training, but now it just means Advanced Individual Training. At AIT the soldier learns his or her trade. My Military Occupational Specialty was a Medical Specialist and classes were at Fort Sam Houston, Texas.

After AIT, a soldier is transferred to their contracted Permanent Duty Station, where they go about their jobs with a modicum of ease. No longer are we being trained. At this point, a certain expected behavior has already been formed. At this point, soldiers know the proper military conduct. Sure we bullshitted amongst ourselves when we were not under the watchful eye of those that could court martial our asses. But when it came down to it, we were on the mark when the shit came down the pike.

PT was still mandatory, especially for those of us in the field but compared to the physical aspect of Boot, Permanent Duty Station was a breeze. Drills and inspections were a constant, but once again, by that time everyone knew what was expected of their boots, bunks, locker, uniforms, rooms, or barracks. We also knew the Army accepted no excuses or made no exceptions. The slackers were already weeded out, at least in my circle of friends.

The trouble I was getting into now was always off-base and almost always involved an overindulgence of alcohol. It included, but was not limited to, fights, indecent exposure, disorderly conduct, trespassing, and resisting and fleeing. The MPs knew me by name, it seemed.

Before my enlistment was up, I injured my left knee. In clinical terms, due to a traumatic lateral subluxation of the left patella, my tibio-femoral joint was unstable. In the eyes of the United States Army, I became physically unfit to serve. When I initially enlisted, I made the mistake of listing an accident I previously had involving my left knee. Because of the disclosure, the Army felt that they did not cause the medical situation but rather aggravated a pre-existing injury. It all adds up to an honorable discharge with no benefits.

They gave me a plane ticket voucher back to Miami, by way of Atlanta (go figure) and two meal tickets. The Army returned my civilian clothes back to me. I cannot begin to tell you how beautiful blues looked. When all you see are greens and brown, blues and reds look like the rainbow itself. I felt awkward being out of uniform, but super excited to be going home.

I sat there at the terminal gate. As I looked around me I caught the eye of this youngster (appearing to be about seventeen–eighteen years old.) She was looking straight at me. I just looked back at her, or maybe, looked *through* her. I guess in thinking back, I was trying to communicate with her, "So what are you about?" "What's your angle?" She looked to the left, to the right, and then sheepishly looked down. I thought, still glaring at her, "Hmm (knitted brow), what was that all about?" It was then that I realized something might have happen to me; something might have changed with me. Were people possibly looking at me the way I looked at them when I first came through Atlanta? "Ah who gives a fuck, anyway?"

Mom and Dad met me at Miami International Airport. They both gave me huge hugs. Something I hadn't felt in quite a while. This was the comfort zone I had longed for but gave up on feeling ever again. I had shut myself off to cope with the reality of my living hell. Mom, seeing my cold façade, asked, "Sweetheart, happy to be home?" Without processing my words, thoughts or present company, I said. "Hell yes, I am glad to be out of that *fucking* Army."

Oops!

Mom gasped. They looked at each other. "Oh my!"

It was as if I was outside my body. I knew where I was but not who I was. Who I had become didn't match where I was standing. Where before, who I became actually meshed with where I was. Does that make sense?

I tried to think of what was now appropriate and what was not. I couldn't remember. I went home to what seemed like a world with no rules. I didn't know what to do. There was no plan; no duty assignment. I had choices in what to wear every day; choices I didn't feel comfortable in making. I didn't know what time to get up. I felt a need to be told where to go and the purpose of the day. Light conversations were difficult for me. It all seemed so stupid and trivial. Voices seemed extra soft and I felt everyone was talking to each other like babies. I couldn't help calling Dad and Mom *Sir* and *Ma'am*. Anyway, it took a while and a lot of patience on the part of my parents. For a few months after coming home, I worked construction before I enrolled at the university.

Do I hate the Army? Well, it made me the person I am today. So no, I do not hate the Army. I am confident, strong and disciplined beyond words. My word is my bond and people around me respect me for that. It is a code of honor. You see, trust is a virtue. I may have learned it in the field with the rest of my buddies. You need to trust the person beside you. Your life depends on their actions. Fuck up once and your word is forever shot. Equating that to civilian life: let's say you have arranged a business meeting and people rearranged their schedule to accommodate you. You cancel because of whatever. From that day forward your word does not mean crap. You are less in their eyes. Whether they articulate that to you or not. O.K., so no one is dead, but trust is forever lost. On the other hand, when you earn the trust of your subordinates and lead by example, they, your subordinates, will respect you and believe or not, follow you. They may even go to bat for you. Trust is earned; not given, and easily broken beyond repair.

Because of my experience "in," my home and office are spotless. This is where my contemporaries consider me anal. Hell, I am not dictating how they should have their place. I just prefer to have my zipper all the way up. I function better and think clearer when things are in their place as well as have purpose. They say my posture when walking and standing is quite erect. Whatever.

I no longer use drugs. I dried out after my return home. I still smoke tobacco though; a habit I picked up while "in." A pack today may last me around three days, where while "in" I was a two packer. My drinking I guess could be curtailed a bit but my tolerance is high, it tastes so damn good, and I feel terrific, so shit, man. I suppose life makes it so easy for me to do justice to a bottle of Scotch.

Every year I try to clean up my language. It seems like so many colorful expressions came out of the Alabama woods or from the barracks that sometimes there is just no other way to truly get across the point without some form of adult expression. I am working on that though.

I am proud, for the most part, of who I am and what I stand for. I am proud of my accomplishments and fortunate to still be able to function after my experience "in."

O.K., would I do it again? HELL, NO. Do I regret my decision to enlist? No I do not.

The intent of this story is not to pass judgement. It is merely to inform you, the reader, of what takes place behind the guarded gate of the U.S. Army. It is to pose questions. It is to give you insight on why ex-Army soldiers, as me, may think, behave or react the way we do. Most of you are quick to vote or argue on the silliness of the whole *discipline* thing of the military or in hearing about wartime atrocities are quick to vote on reform. Please take a step back, re-evaluate and take a look at the bigger picture. Power comes at a price. Discipline, and the resulting, *One is none, Two is one* mentality is necessary for cohesiveness of platoon, the unit and yes, the entire Army. For without it, fragmentation would dilute the power and effectiveness needed for successful completion of the military objectives.

Make your own call. Do you enjoy your country's freedom and safety? Do you know what it takes to retain what we so flippantly call *freedom*?

If America were not a military giant, who would be? Will restructuring the military weaken the soldier, weaken the military as a whole, and weaken our nation? How much training is too much training? It seems it is a question of robotic killers versus the opinionated masses.

Is there a need for brainwashing? Is there a need for a chain of command? Where does one draw the line? How can an instructor get 100 percent from a recruit? Asking, telling, frightening, beating? Where are the boundaries?

Should women be trained to fight, or to support? Should men train women? Can women train men? Do you condone rape? How does one define *abuse of power*?

Where do you stand?

Do you care?

Should you care?

Is any of this justified?

www.ingramcontent.com/pod-product-compliance
Lightning Source LLC
Chambersburg PA
CBHW020302290526
45784CB00003B/1331